Noah's Town
Where Animals Reign

by Maury Forman

Noah's Town: Where Animals Reign tells the story of how the descendants of Noah's Ark have integrated themselves in society and have formed a sustainable and growing community. That is until the never expected, once-in-a-lifetime storm causes havoc among residents and tourists. It is up to Maya Morton, a proud and stubborn donkey and the newly appointed economic developer, to rescue her community and guide it to recovery. This fable illustrates that there is nothing more powerful than a community working together to prepare for a disaster before it happens.

cover illustration: Milt Priggee

i

Reviews

Noah's Town is a great example of the important role economic developers play in helping communities and businesses prepare for, respond to, recover from, and become more resilient to disasters. Nobody thinks it will ever happen to them; however, communities need to be prepared for "when" a disaster happens not "if." This cleverly written and often humorous book does a great job illustrating the unique role economic developers have in this process. As the saying goes, "when disaster strikes the time to prepare has passed."

Leann Hackman-Carty, *Business & Economic Recovery Expert and Author of* "Master your Disaster" Calgary, Canada

In *Noah's Town*, Maury Forman offers a crucial economics lesson in the form of an entertaining fable. It's common today for communities to talk about sustainability programs and doing good things for the planet, but few put adequate thought and planning to building internal resilience. *Noah's Town* aptly illustrates the value of rooting economic development in nurturing local entrepreneurs and building self-reliance. Like all good fables, its lesson is timeless!

Jeff Milchen, *Co-director*
American Independent Business Alliance, Bozeman Montana

Noah's Town has brilliantly tied different aspects of economic development together with the one that most communities forget – preparing for a disaster. If this humorous but serious story does not compel you and your community to prepare, I am not sure what will. The reader will be entertained, educated and energized to turn any disaster into opportunities for a speedy recovery.

Dale Wheeldon, *President and CEO*
British Columbia Economic Development Association, Vancouver, Canada

Throughout the economic development profession, Maury Forman is known for his creativity and wit. He is dedicated to advancing the field by focusing on sustainable growth based on existing businesses, small firms and innovation. In this amazing fable, he has combined that dedication with the newest risk factor that has crippled growth in many communities – disaster risk. That risk is growing, and requires decisive action. In this fable about a magical town where Noah's Ark landed, he weaves a fascinating tale that is both engaging and educational, bringing place-based development and disaster resilience together. As a fellow proponent of sustainable development and resilience, I am thrilled to endorse this book, and plan to purchase it in bulk for my leadership and clients.

David A. Dodd, *Founding President and CEO*
International Sustainable Resilience Center, New Orleans, Louisiana

Foreword

I have been thinking about writing this book for over a decade. But I have actually been thinking about disasters since I was 11 when Hurricane Carla hit my hometown in Galveston Texas in 1961. It was then that I realized the damage and fear that resulted from a natural disaster.

Back then we called them "once in a lifetime" storms. The last big Galveston storm prior to Carla took place in 1900 and killed 12,000 people. That was a lifetime ago. But now natural disasters are part of our lives. They come in all different forms. Barely a day goes by where we don't read about the devastation of floods, hurricanes, tornadoes, volcanic eruptions, earthquakes, tsunamis, and other geologic processes. In the past two decades alone there have been 6,873 natural disasters worldwide, which claimed 1.35 million lives. In addition, 218 million people were affected by natural disasters on average per annum during this 20-year period

If you are an economic developer or elected official, you believe that the worst thing that can happen to a community is that your primary employer relocates to another community. Or maybe a Wal-Mart will come to town and destroy your small business community. Or the reputation of your town gets national negative press because an unfortunate incident occurs. These are all serious issues that can ruin a community's economy and its resident's lives. But fortunately, most communities have recovered from those incidents.

But no, the worst thing that could happen to a community is not to be prepared for a natural disaster. As every citizen knows, we have very little power to prevent these events. But we can take steps to minimize their impact by preparing a community and its businesses to recover quickly. Disasters may be part of our world these days, but their catastrophic impact can be managed to a great extent.

The true test of a community's character is in how its people respond in times of crisis.

As economic developers, it can be tempting to think of crisis planning being a luxury or someone else's job. But as we've learned clearly in the last few years, it is our job and we need to start right now, before the news coverage fades and we return to our daily routines of recruitment, retention and expansion. As the old saying goes, "It wasn't raining when Noah built the ark". Focus on disaster preparation so your businesses won't think of business relocation.

The economic developer's role is to make a difference for local businesses by pushing the economy toward a faster recovery. Retention visits and surveys should include business recovery strategies to help companies prepare for and weather a disaster so people can get back to work as soon as possible. The goal is to not only restore the local economy, but to restore some normalcy to the lives and livelihoods of workers and prevent the bad from getting worse.

It is the intention of this book to recognize that your town could be like Noah's Town, happy and prosperous with a booming economy. Then one day, that "once in a lifetime" event occurs. When disaster strikes in a community, the community has to be prepared to rely on itself. Yes, state and federal resources will eventually make their way into town, but in the hours, days and even weeks following a disaster, you will be on your own. And the question from an economic developer's perspective is, "Are you ready?"

In addition to reading this book, I would like to suggest three excellent sources of information and assistance to help your town prepare and recover. The International Economic Development Council in conjunction with the US Economic Development Administration developed *Restore Your Economy* (http://restoreyoureconomy.org/). This website provides resources and best practice information for public and private stakeholders who are seeking to rebuild their local economies after an economic disruption.

The second valuable resource is *Master Your Disaster: Your Readiness, Response and Recovery Guide*. In this unique well-written guide, preparedness and recovery expert Leann Hackman-Carty shows you how to prepare your family, business, and community for a number of devastating scenarios.

Every community understands the importance of public and private partnerships. And when it comes to disaster preparation and recovery there is no better organization bringing private pubic partnerships together to offset the growing threat of disasters than International Sustainable Resilience Center. They are located in New Orleans but working all over the world supporting recovery efforts when disaster strikes.

Noah was lucky. He didn't have to worry about business failures, power outages, failed wastewater collection or lack of water. Unfortunately, we do. The entire world probably won't be wiped away at once, but as we all know, our entire community can be turned on its end in a single day.

But as Noah discovered, there is a rainbow at the end of all this doom and gloom. For in the end, we all have the ability to control the impact of a disaster. We can be ready for its eventuality and minimize its impact by doing the necessary planning before it strikes, so that in its aftermath, we can focus on recovery rather than wonder what to do next as the world crumbles around us.

Chapter 1

WELCOME TO NOAH'S TOWN

Life was good in Noah's Town, this quaint tourist community, far off the beaten path from the hubbub of everyday life. In some ways, Noah's Town was much like every other small town competing for stature and prosperity. They believed in buying and investing locally and created opportunities that would bring in outside dollars. In fact, for the last several years, Noah's Town was named the "Best Place to Visit."

But Noah's Town was unique from all other communities that competed for the tourist dollar. It was started eons ago when the Ark first settled down on the nearby mountain slopes after the Great Flood where animals roamed aimlessly in their new setting. But as the years passed, Noah's Town was established and inhabited by the descendants of Noah's Ark who lived in harmony with each other. This diverse group of animals learned how to speak a common language and communicate with people from other communities. They also developed skills and became entrepreneurs in their own right. The descendants celebrated the freedom of private ownership and created a healthy community for animal kind.

Economically, it was a perfect storm, not to make light of the town's origins. The surrounding animal-owned farms supplied the town with almost everything its residents needed, from the sheep's wool that went into the coats, hats and gloves that were so popular, to the locally-sourced ingredients used in restaurants that brought visitors from far and wide.

Weekends were a particularly joyous time in Noah's Town. From early spring to late fall, tourists would pack the town, enjoying the fine foods, homemade and locally-sourced goods and appreciating the innocence found in the town's offspring.

Inevitably, impromptu games would begin on the fields at the edge of town, with the calves, cubs, kits, pups, piglets, colts, and whelps engaging in all sorts of fun.

Tourists from all over the country would come to revel in the peace and tranquility found in Noah's Town, watching in delight as creatures of the two- and four-legged variety joined in the games as the doves and crows flew overhead, carrying the message from their founding fathers:

The best thing to spend on your children is time.

As harvest season approached, the community shifted into high gear, making ready for the hard winter days to come while celebrating their blessings in the annual harvest festival. For centuries, the fall festival was the highlight of the year, bringing in visitors and dollars from afar. Hotels and inns were booked a year in advance, such was the popularity of this annual celebration.

One of the highlights of the festival was the special production of the story of the Great Flood, which took place in the massive ark-shaped, state-of-the-art surround-sound theater at the end of town. Nearly everyone in Noah's Town was involved in the production in one way or another. Some playing the many animals and insects kept on the Ark, others building sets, doing the marketing and finding parking for all the cars that brought visitors to town.

For more than two and a half hours, the audience would sit enraptured, not only marveling at the story as depicted in The Bible, but also the theater, which looked like it could float away at any moment. It looked so authentic and seaworthy. Theater-goers experienced an incredible journey as they were strapped in their seats and swept across the floodwaters to a new world that included amazing sights, sweet and pungent smells, and the feeling of wind and mist on their faces. It's as if they were really there.

The climax of the play was the part when the waters receded and the story of Noah's Town was told. Amid a rising chorus of song, as the play drew to a close, the audience would always rise to their feet and offer a standing ovation to the actors and town folk who made the story come to life.

As the audience left the theater through the large gangways along the sides of The Ark, many people found themselves in no hurry to go home, as Noah's Town offered so many wonderful diversions that it was hard to leave.

Visitors could just leave their cars in the lot and catch a shuttle to town where they could get a bite to eat, shop for souvenirs and enjoy a slice of small town life.

Downtown was worth the visit.

There was Swannee's Souvenirs, which was owned by a beautiful swan whose artistic talents allowed her to recreate facsimiles of many of the artifacts on display in the Ark.

Legend has it – and Swannee would neither confirm nor deny – that her great-great-great-great-great-great-great-great-great-great grandmother was the one who sang the final song aboard the Ark as the animals emerged two by two. Yes, today it's still referred to as a swan song.

Next door was the Mooseum, which traced the history of Noah's Town. Morris, the museum's antlered curator and an amateur ark-eologist, loved telling stories of how the town's founders survived the Great Flood. Morris was a natural choice to run the Mooseum. He loved to give impromptu tours, proudly showing the Mooseum's tableaus of early pioneer life.

Another popular stop for tourists was Glenda's Golden Eggs. Glenda was relatively new to town having relocated relatively late in her life. She and her elderly geese seniors flew down from Canada one summer and she instantly fell in love with Noah's Town. This is where she decided she would spend the rest of her life.

The townsfolk readily embraced her as one of their own, if for no other reason than they found her halting, honking speech and constant use of the word "eh" at the end of every sentence endearing. She opened up her own restaurant and Noah's Town residents and visitors flocked to Glenda's Golden Eggs as she served the best egg dishes within a hundred miles. It included not only eggs-quisite preparation but also egg-ceptional presentation. Patrons left her restaurant not only with their bellies full but also with a smile as they waddled under a sign that said "Eggs-it.

Next door was Snooze, You Lose Sports. It was run by two famous friends, a tortoise and a hare, whose great-greats opened the store after a very famous race between them. Many visitors are amazed to learn the famed race was really about competing business plans, not speed. The hare had a high-growth strategy. The tortoise, for his part, wanted to take a slower, more predictable route. It was agreed that whoever lost the race would put up the cash and the winner would get to use his business plan.

On the historic day, they set off and as we all know, the tortoise beat the hare by several hairs, though the hare's heirs continue to dispute this fact – there are plenty of hares' heirs who still want to split hairs about who actually won.

A banner over the cash register still reminds everyone of the race results:

Success is a journey, not a destination. Stop running.

Across the street from the sporting goods store stands Three Bags Full, run by entrepre-animals, Sammy and Mary Shears. The black sheep of the family, Sammy was ostracized by the flock when he married Mary, whose fleece was white as snow. They had just welcomed a new addition to the family, and sure enough, wherever Mary went, the lamb was sure to go.

Three Bags Full not only produced sustainable winter wear in the softest wool around, but he also had a successful repair business on the side, mending wool socks, jerseys and sweaters. Whenever the little children brought their clothes to mend, they would ask Sammy if "he had any wool" and Sammy would dutifully answer, "Yes sir, yes sir, three bags full." Everyone in the shop would laugh and Sammy would guffaw in a most outlandish way that made everyone else laugh harder.

Not bad for a guy who was really quite sheepish.

The economy in Noah's Town was indeed booming. New opportunities abounded, in part because the town had grown over the years without a centralized plan. To the residents, it was all God-given and the natural order of things. Who were they to interfere with God's plan.

New businesses joined existing ones from time to time along Main Street. One of the newer businesses in town was Kneed to Know. An orangutan family, the curious Georges, fell in love with Noah's Town during their last vacation. Their most popular product was banana bread, a recipe learned from his father, making him a chimp off the old block. The aroma of the bread drew in a constant stream of shoppers. Each morning there was a line down the block in front of the store as locals and visitors queued up to get a piping hot loaf of fresh bread. While waiting in line they were entertained with a riddle of the day. Today's riddle was "What did the bag of flour say to the loaf of banana bread?" The answer would print out on the receipt. Today, it was "I saw you yeasterday." Some people groaned while others laughed. Some paused a bit, and then said, "Oh, I get it."

About the only thing visitors couldn't find in Noah's Town was a good butcher shop. Many, many years ago, the town was embroiled in something of a scandal. A couple visiting the town were rumored to have disappeared mysteriously without a trace. Fingers of blame were pointed at the lions and tigers and bears, oh my, but they were clearly not to blame. It turned out the couple had merely gotten lost as they hiked the trails in the surrounding hills.

Eventually the bad press faded away but local officials, not wishing to stir up any further controversy, declared that all restaurants and shops in city limits would be meat free.

It was a brilliant move but the feud between the lions and tigers continued with the tigers saying the lions were lying and the lions calling the tigers cheetahs.

With confidence restored, tourists readily flocked back to the town and gave rave reviews about the new restaurant fare that came from the small farms surrounding the town. Even when the official tourist season was over, the new dining experiences continued to be popular with residents and the ability to enjoy and then buy locally grown products created a year round economic stability, something the town welcomed with open arms.

This even led one wag to post a sign in the dead of night on the edge of Main Street that read:

No animals or humans were harmed when feeding our guests.

It was quite the talk of the town the next morning when Morris found it on the way to the Mooseum. But the townsfolk quickly took a shine to it and it's been there ever since.

Glenda and the Georges weren't the only outsiders to end up calling Noah's Town home. The community's low crime, good schools and tranquil quality of life made it an attractive place to be. The economy grew steadily and predictably while the influx of new residents afforded the townsfolk the opportunity to find gainful employment and living wage jobs.

The Chamber of Commerce had a field day with this influx of new workers and residents. Their marketing campaign, which was shared around the world, was captured in a single sign in front of the Chamber office:

Noah's Town: A place you don't have to leave
to get away from it all.

That certainly captured the sentiment of the town. People arrived in droves, usually in twos, which delighted Morris and others familiar with the town's history. It didn't delight the town's singles, however, who found it almost impossible to find a match since most newcomers were already paired up.

To spur further economic growth, they instituted an incubator and workspace program to tap into the existing wealth of talent in town and promote innovation among the youth. When the incubator program was launched, the town's council tapped Charlie to run it even though he was no spring chicken. He had actually been born in an incubator so the mayor figured he would be a natural for the role. Charlie was not really sure how to grow entrepreneurs but he decided to just wing it.

Charlie quickly warmed up to the idea, and he dove enthusiastically into the incubator program, diligently building it without ruffling any feathers, including his own. He hatched a strategic plan after the first year that provided technical assistance for the program, helping its entrepreneurs to stand on their own two- or four-feet without being cocky. It didn't take long to see that the town council made a wise decision. What he lacked in experience he succeeded with wisdom.

One of his biggest successes was Straw, Sticks and Bricks, a construction business that was responsible for almost all the new construction in Noah's Town over the last few years. It could be said, and had been said by a few of the town's planners, that the three brothers were total pigs,

6

taking advantage of lax construction and housing requirements so they could put up their inexpensive buildings without much interference from the inspector.

Who could really blame them for the building inspector, Willy Wolf, was a real stickler for following the rules and when they weren't followed, he huffed and puffed about it for days.

Charlie was nearing retirement age. Still, his years in economic development and first hand experience with incubators gave him tremendous insight and knowledge, something that would be hard to replace.

As a member of the economic development community for so many years, his opinion carried a lot of weight in town. And though things seemed to be going swimmingly in Noah's Town, he fretted from time to time, worrying that the sky was falling, or soon would be. He didn't want to cause alarm, but he worried that things were just too good to be true and that no one wanted to think about what would or could happen if something went wrong.

Who could blame the town's officials or even the residents? Times were good in Noah's Town. Rooms were regularly sold out for weekends. The Ark was drawing record crowds, business was brisk and money was rolling into the town's coffers. It was hard to imagine anything bad happening; times were too good to spend time worrying.

Chapter 2

HOME SWEET HOME?

It was summer time in Noah's Town. That meant not only were the streets flooded with tourists but also college students were returning home for vacation, visiting friends and looking for jobs.

Maya Morton was one of those students returning home for a short visit after her college graduation. She held the honor of becoming the school's first valedictorian and was also the first Noah's Town resident to graduate with such an honor. Maya was looking forward to seeing her friends and family before returning to the big city to seek a well-paying job fresh from receiving her degree in business.

As Maya drove down Main Street, all the memories came flooding back to her. She had grown up in Noah's Town. She hadn't been back since she headed off to college, but nothing much had changed. It was as if time had stood still.

Like most kids in town, Maya graduated from Naaman High School which was named after Noah's wife, who believed that education was the key to success. Her school even gave all its students a small plaque at graduation that said:

Education is the most powerful weapon which you can use to change the world.

Maya loved that quote. She wanted to change the world.

Her parents desperately wanted her to go into the family business when she finished school, but Maya wanted to see what the outside world looked like before settling down and making her mark.

Maya's stubbornness came naturally. You might even say it was something of a family trait, given that she came from a long line of proud yet stubborn donkeys.

From an early age, Maya knew what she wanted out of life. When she set her mind to it, there was nothing anyone could do to stop her.

The town had changed little over the last four years. To Maya, fresh out of business school, this was both comforting and alarming. While in college, she had done an internship with a nearby community, working in their economic development office. It was there she fell in love with the craft, the gentle art and science of guiding a community's economic vitality, developing a skilled workforce, providing technical assistance to entrepreneurs, helping startups find financing and attracting the occasional investment from new players who saw potential in a small town.

She enjoyed the profession so much that she even took courses offered by the International Economic Development Council and paid for it with her own money. At their conferences and workshops she networked with many people from around the country who were implementing innovative strategies in their communities. It was a dream job even if it did not pay very well or lasted only a few years.

The internship had been Charlie's idea. Charlie had been a friend of the family for as long as Maya could remember and he had pulled a few strings to get her the internship.

His impending retirement was one of the reasons Maya had returned to Noah's Town. It was to be a brief visit, a send off for a good friend who had helped her decide on her major. How could she not attend his retirement party and thank him for the opportunities he had given her?

She pulled in front of Al Capachino's. It was new since the last time Maya had been here, but she was glad the town finally had a decent coffee shop. She liked the idea of having locally grown businesses in Noah's Town. Visitors would come to see or buy something they could not get in their own hometown and Noah's Town offered plenty of unique experiences.

Maya waited in line, looking at the photos hung along the wall. They were historic photos from the Mooseum that showed what Al's building looked like through the many decades it has stood in this part of town.

Maya smiled as she was reminded of the candy store that once occupied the space. Many summer afternoons she and her brother Mueller spent their allowance there on sweets and ice cream.

As she sipped her double tall latte skinny, no foam, she noticed something else unique. Her cup had a cleverly written message for the day. It read:

If you feel depresso, have a little espresso.

Maya loved seeing the feel good, pun-filled messages that appeared on the cups and throughout the town. She felt it gave residents and tourists a positive message about living and being in Noah's Town. As she left Al's, she thought to herself, Thanks a latte. She laughed out loud at her own pun.

Maya looked out on Main Street with a fresh perspective. Yes, she had grown up here, but now she saw Noah's Town through the eyes of an economic developer. The town was very charming, she thought, even picturesque. Any other place would love to have its problems.

Problems?

Parking for one, she thought. Main Street was mostly one-hour parking. Longer term parking was on the secondary streets behind the Main Street and all-day lots were out near the Ark. There were shuttle buses that ran into town from those lots, but finding parking for a quick errand or two if you're a resident was a bit of a task. Even Maya had a hard time finding an open spot along Main Street. Fortunately, someone had pulled out of their spot in front of Al's just as she rounded the corner on her second loop around. Discovering an empty parking space often took longer than the errand itself.

The weather seemed troublesome too — not that anyone could do anything about it. But the mountains surrounding Noah's Town had a way of trapping the weather when the winds were just right.

In the summer, this was a blessing, for the skies would be clear for weeks on end. Given the altitude, it was never too hot in Noah's Town and this was a huge draw for tourists wanting to escape the heat of the big city on a sultry summer's day.

In the winter, it would snow. Not so much that the passes were impossibly impassible. Just enough to give the town a lovely blanket of white that fueled the holiday season traffic. The community held its annual street and tree lighting along Main Street, complete with bands in the gazebo and a nightly appearance of Santa and his reindeer.

The shoulder seasons were more problematic. The weather could never seem to make up its mind. One day it would be warm and sunny, the next, a torrential downpour of biblical proportions.

Today was one of those confusing weather days. It started out to be 'chamber of commerce' gorgeous. But as she continued her stroll down memory lane on Main Street, it started to rain

The rain had turned into something of a deluge. Big drops pounded on the pavement in front of Al Capachino's. Maya couldn't remember a time when it rained with such conviction. The gutters running along Main Street could barely keep up with all the water.

Maya was in no hurry to make many stops in this weather. Thankfully, Charlie's incubator space was just across the street. If she timed it right, she could dash across without getting too much of a drenching.

She finished her latte, grabbed her umbrella and purse. She stood briefly in the doorway, looking for the traffic to create an opportunity, then darted across the street, leaping over the now full gutter. A brilliant dance she thought as she started across Main Street, dodging drops, puddles and traffic. Halfway across, the wind suddenly picked up and turned her umbrella inside out. It spun her a bit in the wind. She fought the elements bravely, finally making it to the door of the incubator.

Charlie was waiting for her inside.

"I don't remember it raining like this, Charlie," she said, unbuttoning her raincoat.

"Well, at least it's not raining 40 days and 40 nights… yet," he replied.

They both laughed.

"Long time no see, stranger," Maya said after taking a seat across from Charlie in his office. "What's been going on since I left town?"

"Same ol', same ol," Charlie said. "You know small towns. Nothing much changes around here. About the only thing people talk about these days is the weather."

Charlie and Maya talked for almost an hour. Charlie loved to tell stories about when Maya was growing up and how she was always curious about one thing or another.

"Looks like you haven't changed much, Maya. I'm glad. A lot of the local kids never come back here after they've been out in that big world of ours. They want to be where the action is, life in the big city where there's plenty of opportunities but very little..."

"Soul?" Maya said, finishing Charlie's thought.

"You said it Maya, not me. As you know, I am calling it a career finally. I think this may be an opportunity for you."

"What's left to do here?" Maya said. "The town is bustling, storefronts are full, dollars are flowing in and we have hardly any unemployment. It looks like thumb twiddling time."

Charlie tipped back in his chair, his wings tucked behind his head.

"Do you think this all happens by magic, Maya? What do you think I've been doing around here all these years?"

"Why, helping entrepreneurs start businesses at the incubator, of course," she shot back.

"Towns that run themselves without someone to guide them is a town that runs amok. I've spent the better part of 30 years here now, working behind the scenes to help make sure our lovely community continues to grow intelligently, that we have a workforce that matches the needs of businesses, working on projects to improve Main Street and infrastructure..."

"Can you say, economic development?" Maya said.

"And with me heading off to roost, it's a good time for new blood to take over so we can elevate this work to a higher level. I think you should speak with the mayor about creating an economic development function within the town's government."

"Really?" Maya said. "I had planned to leave Noah's Town in the rear view mirror. I know it way too well, like the back of my hoof. It doesn't seem like a smart career move."

"That's why you're perfect. In fact, you have a 10 o'clock tomorrow with the mayor," Charlie replied. "I took the liberty of making it for you. Now, don't feel any pressure about it. Just talk to her about Noah's Town. The answers will come to you."

Chapter 3

YOU WANT TO DO WHAT?

When Maya arrived at the mayor's office the next morning, the office was abuzz. Staff were running around the office frantically, clucking and chirping about some problem in town.

Maya wondered if it all had something to do with the terrible rainstorm during the night. Main Street was awash as the drainage system was overwhelmed with all the water. There was nowhere for it to go.

She tried to eavesdrop on the conversations around her, but they simply blended into the cacophony of a barnyard choir. Everyone was talking at once, but no one seemed to be listening. Something was definitely afoot.

Maya was sure the mayor would find a reason, any reason, not to take this meeting.

Mare was the town's mayor, almost by accident. She had been employed in the town's blanket factory before it folded.

She was out of work with no prospects on the horizon. At the time, she was a very slim horse due to being on a stable diet. As she was getting a drink from the local watering trough one day, she heard someone say, "Who was the mare?"

Well, that's what she thought they said. Being a bit deaf from working all day with the noisy blanket-making machinery, Mare replied, "Me."

The visitor was really asking "who was the mayor" but by now the die was cast. From then on, the old gray mare, who was not what she used to be, became the de facto head of Noah's Town.

Part of the reason there wasn't much progress in Noah's Town was because Mayor Mare wasn't exactly progressive. It wasn't necessarily her fault. At town meetings the mayor would dutifully bring up any new business to be considered, but when it came time to vote, she always said, "Nay," not because she was against the idea, but because horses don't have the ability to say, "Yay!"

She was surprised when at five minutes after the hour the mayor's assistant ushered Maya through the door.

"Good morning, Maya," the mayor said, not looking up from some papers she was signing. "What can I do for you?"

"I would like to discuss the creation of a position within the town to…"

The mayor cut her off.

"Do economic development, right? At least that's what Charlie told me. Look Miss Morton. We don't really need someone to sit around here all day and play with numbers, making predictions about where the economy is going. The idea's laughable at best."

"Speaking of laughs, did you hear this one?" the mayor continued. "Economists are the only profession where you can become eminent without ever being right. Get it?"

The mayor laughed long and hard.

Maya was unfazed. "Madam Mayor, economic developers are not number crunchers or prognosticators. Economic developers focus on people and businesses. They help communities grow, address potential threats to the economic wealth of a community, align workforce with the needs of business and ensure that there's proper infrastructure to handle predicted growth."

"Look around you, Maya. Does it look like our business community needs any help?" the mayor replied. "People love Noah's Town. Tourists come to spend their money and business is booming. And our Festival of the Ark was just named the 48th Best Festival in the entire country.

"48th? Are you proud of that?," Maya said. "Do you promote Noah's Town with 'We're 48th best in the country?' Why would anyone choose to go to the 48th best festival when they could go to 47 others that are rated better? Don't you want to be #1?"

The mayor stared blankly at her, silent.

Without a breath, Maya continued. "Of all the tourists who visit Noah's Town, how many are returning versus how many are here for the first time? Are there gaps in the types of businesses in the community that can be filled with new business ideas? Are the incubator businesses staying in town or are they relocating somewhere else after Charlie certifies them as business ready? What does the next generation need from Noah's Town to stay here after graduation and contribute to the community they grew up in rather than leave? And what happens if there's a disaster that affects the town? Did you see downtown this morning? The streets are flooded."

Maya couldn't believe her own ears. She didn't come here to get a job. She had different plans. But there she was, pitching a position with the town's administration.

The mayor's smile faded. "Whoa! Hold your horses, Ms. Big City Girl. Of course I'm aware. I'm sure you've seen all the hustle and bustle around here. We're dealing with it. It's not like it rained for 40 days and 40 nights. Recently. We are more than prepared to handle a hundred-year flood. Our Public Works Director Vern assures me that the recent rains are just an aberration. It's nothing to worry about."

Maya's stubbornness kicked in. "Well, what if there's a 500-year storm? Or a thousand year one? Or worse, what if the tourists start hearing about our flooding problems and decide to vacation elsewhere. I would guess that 65 percent of the economy is based on tourism."

"Well, your guess would be wrong, Maya. More like 70 percent."

"You do know, Madam Mayor, that a thousand-year flood doesn't mean that it happens once every thousand years. You can have one tomorrow, and another a year from now. In fact, there have been 24 'thousand-year storms' since 2010 in this country."

"Where did you get that little tidbit from," the mayor said, growing testy.

"USA Today," Maya shot back. "There was a story on it just last week."

"I really like that newspaper," the mayor replied. "So colorful and…"

"Stay with me, Madam Mayor. As I said, the term doesn't mean that you'll have a flood of that scale every 1,000 years. It means that there is a

1 in 1,000 chance you'll have flooding each year. Insurers and emergency responders use it to measure the danger of flooding in a particular area."

"Now you do sound like an economist," the mayor said. "Speaking of economists, how many economists does it take to change a light bulb?"

"Mayor, I don't see how this…" Maya interjected.

"Seven, plus or minus ten. I got a million of these, Maya." The mayor whinnied for the longest time.

Maya decided to change her approach.

"Madam Mayor, what's the biggest problem facing Noah's Town today, besides a flooded Main Street."

"Creating more living wage jobs, I would guess. The town has been growing by leaps and bounds as of late. Ever since that rabbit family moved into town we've experienced explosive growth because they breed like . . ."

"Rabbits?" Maya said. "I get it."

"So, can you create more jobs, Miss Economic Developer?" the mayor chided, miffed that Maya stepped on her punch line.

"No, I don't create jobs. That's not what economic developers do, Madam Mayor. But what I can do is work with businesses and community groups to create a healthy landscape that will lead to more diversification, more cultural and social activities, and more job opportunities, including those that go beyond catering to tourists."

"There's nothing wrong with catering to tourists, Missy."

"Maya. The name is Maya, not Missy. Look, there's nothing wrong with tourism as an industry or even as the major economic driver of a community. But don't you want some diversity, so should the number of visitors taper off there are other businesses or entire sectors that can take up the slack? Diversity will help strengthen the community by spreading the risk around. Plus, it will give the town's youth more opportunities to stay since they can find work in fields that interest them rather than shoehorning their dreams into the tourist trade, which aren't exactly known for their high pay."

"You've brought up some good points Maya, I must say," the mayor said. "I'll roll it around a bit and talk to some of the folks on the council. I'll get back to you on this. Right now, I have a briefing to attend on the flooding."

"Thank you, Ms. Mayor. I look forward to hearing from you."

"One more thing," the mayor said, shaking her hand at the door. "Why was astrology invented?"

"Why?"

"So economics would seem like an exact science."

Maya rolled her eyes and smiled. She could still hear the mayor whinnying as she walked down the hall and out the door.

Maya shook her head. She didn't plan to pitch herself for any role in economic development here. She wasn't planning to return to Noah's Town. She was just trying to be polite, since Charlie set the meeting up. But then again, it was an opportunity to do what she loved, in a town that she still loved deep down.

The next day, Maya got a call from the mayor.

"This is Mayor Mare. I talked it over with some of the town council and we've decided to let you do your little economic development thing on a trial basis. I'd like you to come to the council meeting on Tuesday so we can formalize the role and you can meet some of the town's movers and shakers."

"I'll be there," Maya said, trying to keep her composure and hide her surprising excitement.

Maya entered the council's meeting room promptly at 7 p.m. There was already a hubbub going on before the meeting was even called to order. The building inspector, Willy Wolf, was in a heated discussion with the three pigs about their shoddy building practices. Ali Gator was keeping them separated, trying to keep the peace. Earlier in the day, Willy had huffed and puffed at a new build at the edge of town and blew the house away. Needless to say, it didn't pass his rigorous inspection process. The pigs were squealing loudly about his methods.

Mayor Mare finally brought order to the meeting with the rap of her gavel and her raspy voice. "Excuse me," she said taking a sip of water, "I am a little hoarse today."

Maya was the first item of New Business the town had had in quite some time so the council chamber was packed with spectators.

"And now we have the matter of our new Economic Development Director. Council member Hereford moo'ved that we appoint Maya Morton to the position on a trial basis. Do we have a second?"

"Second," said one of the other council members.

"Maya, would you like to come up here and answer any questions the council or the public may have for you before we bring this to a vote?"

Maya stepped up to the podium, ready to field all of the questions the council undoubtedly would ask her.

Council member Al Paca spoke first, but not before he spat into the spittoon that was next to his seat at the long table before her.

"Miss Morton. I think I speak for the entire council when I say that we look forward to you joining us on this trial basis. I have just one question to ask," he said, spitting again. "Just how many jobs are you going to create here in Noah's Town? Feel free to frame your answer by the week, by the month, or whatever metric you economists use."

Maya took a long breath. This was not starting out well. Or maybe it was just to be expected, given the Mayor's viewpoint.

"Council member Paca. First, it's good to see you again. It's been awhile, hasn't it, and here you don't look a day older than when I left town four years ago."

Al smiled back at her, spat once more, then settled back in his chair.

"As I told the mayor, I'm not here to create jobs. I'm here to help the community position itself for the future, to create new opportunities for growth, align workforce with the needs of businesses and hopefully, help this community with any unforeseen issues, such as natural or man-made disasters that may affect our livelihoods, our businesses and our families."

20

"Quite frankly, if I could magically create jobs in a community, any community, I don't think it would be this one."

The room grew silent. The silence was deafening.

"What do you mean, Miss Morton?" the mayor interjected. "And I hope you will choose your words wisely."

"If jobs are all this town needs, then it doesn't need me," Maya said with confidence. "The Ark and a bustling downtown have already done that. And I'm not about to propose that we spend my time, and your money and resources to recruit some outside business here with the promise of investment and jobs when Noah's Town is doing quite well on its own. Why, I know a dozen other towns in this state alone that would love to have the problems we have here. We are lucky to live in such a wonderful place. God was certainly smiling down upon us the day the Ark came to rest on that mountain just above town."

The room erupted with applause. Maya had hit a nerve. She wasn't being false either. She grew up here. She knew why people loved to come to Noah's Town. It's just that it was the last place she thought would mark the start of her career.

Councilman Hereford was moo-ved by the reception from the town attendees and immediately commended Maya for her remarks. "Thank you Ms. Morton for your honesty. I am glad to hear that you did not just give us the same old deja moo. That's the feeling the council gets when we hear the same bull over and over again."

"All in favor of Maya's appointment?" said the mayor. "Are there any Nays?" Everyone laughed knowing that there was always one Nay-sayer in the room, the mayor. She just couldn't help herself.

"The motion is passed and adopted. Congratulations Miss Morton. We will see you tomorrow at 9 sharp in your new office in city hall."

The meeting was adjourned and everyone stayed around to enjoy some refreshments. A couple members of the business community came up to offer Maya their good wishes. The moment felt very good for Maya because too often in her life she had felt seen but not herd. Charlie stood within her line of sight, beaming like a proud father. She couldn't tell if he was happy for her or happy for him, as now he could look forward to his retirement years knowing that all his hard work was in good hands.

21

As Maya greeted yet another well-wisher, she heard a rather obnoxious tapping sound. She turned but didn't see anyone. She turned around again to address some more of the town's business people but the sound continued. She turned again, this time to see a very impatient beaver looking up her.

"Missth Morton," he said, with a slight whistle between his teeth. "I'm the Public Worksth Director, Vern Damitol."

Maya snickered to the point that she let go a small bray, even though she had tried so hard to contain it.

"Ith something funny, Missth Morton? Do I amuse you in some fashion?"

"Oh, no, Mr. Damitol," she said. "You don't amuse me in the least."

"You and I need to have a seriouth dithcussion about this town," he said. "I see things others around here don't, stuff that is a little dithconthert-ing."

"I would love to sit down with you, Mr. Damitol," she said, trying desperately to look and sound professional. "Say early next week, once I get settled in a bit?

"That would be fine, Missth Morton. Fine. Welcome aboard. I know we could use someone like you here. Someone with a fresh perspective."

Chapter 4

A NEW BEGINNING

Morning in a tourist town starts early, too early for Maya's tastes. The hubbub began just after sun break and it was hard for her to ignore its persistence. There was bread to make, meals to prepare, sidewalks to sweep and flowers to water.

As she sat up, looking out the window at the street below, she remembered that this is one of the things she loved about life in a small town. It had a subtle rhythm to it, like the slow rocking of a boat at anchor rather than the wake of a big city cruise liner dictating its own terms to the water surrounding it.

The routine was comforting, not distracting. She lingered at the edge of the bed longer than normal to soak in the start of the day. There would be other days like this, of course. But none like your first day at work in a field you prepared for, studied for, and are so passionate about.

Maya dressed, then bounded down the stairs of the boarding house she was staying in. She had thought about living with her mom and dad at the outskirts of town, but that just seemed a bit too high school for her. She had gotten used to doing her own thing while she was at college and didn't want her parents to mollycoddle her, not when she wanted to be her own person. Especially now that she was heading up economic development for the town.

Most of the storefronts were still shuttered, gently letting early rising tourists know that the town was not quite awake yet. Thankfully, Al Capachino's was already open. She didn't even have to look. The scent of freshly roasted coffee and the aroma of baked pastries were enough.

She could get used to this. It was just like being back in college; those mornings when she and her schoolmates would linger over a latte and scones, talking about what they were going to accomplish once they graduated.

The bell on Al's shop door alerted all to her arrival. At least she thought it was the bell on the door. It was actually Council member Hereford who was trying to bat a fly away from his ear. He seemed to be in a bit of a foul moo'd.

It was going to be a busy first day, so Maya thought an extra jolt from some caffeine would give her the edge she needed as she started her new position.

"A double tall, with three pumps of vanilla, soy milk, please," she said. She heard a snort and the bell ring again. She looked over at Council member Hereford. "Make that whole milk instead."

The message on her coffee on this day was very prescient.

> *Pro-caffeinating: (n) the tendency to not start anything until you've had your coffee*

She was definitely not in her old college town anymore. Maya took a seat near the window and started to map out what her day would be like. There was already a lot on her plate. After filling out the necessary paperwork from HR, she wanted to get started on the survey that she planned to send out to businesses in town. She figured that would be a great way to find out the town's priorities and how she can best serve the businesses and residents.

She was so busy with her planning that she didn't even notice Charlie across from her.

"Already hard at work, I see," he clucked. Maya jumped a bit, momentarily startled.

"Oh, good morning Charlie. I guess I was in my own little world."

"What are you working on so early in the day?" he said, quaffing a piping hot cup of tea.

"A survey for the business community."

Charlie sat silent for a moment.

"Did I say something wrong?" Maya asked.

"No, Maya, nothing. I only offer this one piece of advice. This isn't the city you did your internship in. Each town is different, each has its own quirks, if you will. Noah's Town is a very special place, as you well know. Let it guide you in your efforts. If you do, you'll never go wrong."

With that, Charlie bid her a good morning and got up to leave.

"You'll be just fine, Maya," he said, opening the door. "I know you're going to be wonderful in your new role here."

Maya took another sip of her latte and wondered what Charlie meant. Economic development is just economic development, she thought. The process is the same wherever you go. How much different could Noah's Town be from the larger city she interned with?

She looked at her watch. "Time to go to work," she thought. Don't want to be late on your first day.

Maya crossed the street and headed down the short block that led to the main square. Town Hall was at the far end, its clock tower unmistakable. She bounded up the stairs just as it began to chime eight times.

As she arrived at her office, a pile of paperwork was waiting for her. At the top of each form was a number: I-9. SF-144, W-4, FMS-2231, DL1-65 and dozens more. She started to fill them out but decided to tackle them later so she could begin the work she came to do. She did not want to be a bureaucrat with a number. She wanted to be an activist growing a healthy community.

Setting the forms to one side, Maya was suddenly struck by the fact that she didn't really have a plan. All she had thought of so far was to do a survey of businesses. That was hardly a strategy.

Maybe that was what Charlie was really trying to say when he didn't say anything at all.

No matter. Maya went back to work on her survey. Other staff members passed by her open door, but no one stopped in to say hello or welcome her. Ah, the lonely, secluded life of an economic developer, she thought.

The survey was an easy place to start.

Maya had a number of goals in sending out a survey to all of the businesses listed on the town's rolls. Their responses would guide much of her plan.

- Identify the number and categorize the types of businesses.

- Determine the workforce, training and technical assistance needs of local businesses.

- Assist in scaling up businesses wanting to expand.

- Recognize the challenges that threaten the businesses.

- Establish a disaster preparation plan.

- Show the community's appreciation for its business community.

Maya felt she could ask no more than five questions within each goal. This would give her some baseline data that she could then follow up with during on-site visits. Talking to the businesses she could go a bit more in-depth while giving businesses a better idea of why economic development mattered to Noah's Town.

She programmed it into the computer and clicked the Send button.

"That's one thing off my......."

Before she could even finish her sentence, her computer was dinging like an ice cream truck on a hot summer day. Dozens of emails were appearing on her screen that said: "This email message can not be delivered to Distribution List because the email address is no longer valid."

"Holy Mule…," Maya thought.

And just as she was going to bellow a curse word someone knocked. It was the mayor.

"I want to welcome you to town hall, Maya. Everyone's excited to see what you come up with."

Maya started to say something about the survey she had just sent, but the mayor had already flitted off to her next appointment.

"This is going to be a long day," she thought.

It was. First days in a new job usually are. Especially when you're a new person in a new position. Economic development wasn't part of the thought process around here. Everything in the town had just been chugging right along like a bee sucking nectar from a flower. The town figured the economy would buzz right along as well.

"Like the rain?" she heard someone say. She thought someone was reading her mind.

"Like the rain?" the voice said again. Maya leaned over her desk to see who it was. It was Vern.

"The rain?" she said.

"Yes, the rain, outside. It always makes the town thmell so freth in the early morning. I never get tired of the rain, except when..."

"When what?" Maya asked.

"We'll talk about that later. I've got a meeting with the mayor right now. Bye." Vern turned tail and left as quickly as he appeared.

Maya started to joke to herself about him being as busy as a beaver, but then remembered that he was just that.

Maya checked her email, then checked it, again.

The only responses so far were delivery exceptions. Obviously, the town's email lists were horribly out of date as her once empty inbox was now filling with undeliverable notices.

"Well, there's a project to tackle. I wonder what the rest of the town's digital toolbox looks like," Maya thought.

She decided the first thing she was going to put on her "to do" list was to get correct addresses for the database.

She pulled up the town's website to see how well it was serving as an economic development tool. She knew from her college days and internship that a community often gave their website very little thought when it came to being an effective attraction and retention mechanism. The IT folks rarely thought about making it easier for businesses to find information about permitting or regulations.

In class, she had studied some towns that didn't even address economic development issues, such as investment opportunities, available properties, workforce readiness or infrastructure, or the availability of affordable water or power.

It didn't take long for Maya to realize that Noah's Town was one of those towns. The site wasn't much help at all. It looked like it had been set up several years ago and forgotten.

For the next several hours, she poured through the site, analyzing its navigation and user experience, doing some test searches from the perspective of an existing business or an investor, and surveyed the site from the point of view of a business in another town looking for expansion opportunities.

She jotted all her notes down on a legal pad along with lots of arrows and lines to show how a site should be built with economic development in mind. This included obvious connections between the economic development section (such as it was) and other departments and information business users would expect or need, like permitting.

She finished her day with an appointment request to meet with the webmaster of the town's website to discuss her review.

"Welcome to economic development," she said as she closed her laptop for the day.

The next four days weren't much different. Each day started with logging into her email to see if any surveys had been returned. They hadn't. She checked her calendar for appointments. There were none. No voicemail. No walk-ins.

This is not how she imagined it. As she nursed her morning latte, she decided she had to take another tack. If she didn't, she would either be fired for incompetence or die from sheer boredom. Even Vern had gone underground, which is not unusual for a beaver.

Maya awoke on Saturday in despair. Had she made a mistake taking this job? She was not a quitter though. She would make it work.

First things first. The weather was gorgeous outside and Maya made up her mind to enjoy the day, exploring the town as if she was a visitor. She would try to experience it from a new perspective, hoping this would help her formulate a new economic development strategy for the town.

Rather than following her usual routine of getting up and heading down to Al's, she decided instead to drive to the outskirts of town and follow the stream of visitors back into Noah's Town.

She followed the signs to the large parking lots near the Ark. For tourists, this was often the first stop, and to the town's credit, they seemed to already know that parking downtown and then catching a tram to the Ark was not an option.

"Well, that's a start. Still, I think it would be far better if visitors could park closer to the businesses. I'll definitely add that to the list and have the option to go either way – to the Ark or the main business center.

But that was not the only problem. There was no consistency or clear communication for wayfinding. The sight lines were misplaced, and there was excessive and unnecessary information on the posts to name just a few things that needed to be changed.

If it were not for the fact that the Ark was so big, people would never be able to find it. What was needed was a consistent information system that showed non-residents how to get to the town's main attraction and to the areas where they can spend money.

"So where's the town?" she heard someone say within earshot. "I see the trams to the Ark, but is there a decent cup of coffee around here?"

Maya looked around. The signs pointing to the trams that went to the Ark were easy to spot in the parking lot. But the signs pointing to town – let alone the tram that would take you there – were nowhere to be seen.

"I know a great place in town," said Maya. "Al Capachino's has the best coffee in Noah's Town."

"Is it far? I don't see a downtown anywhere," the visitor replied, as his flock poured from the car.

"There's a tram that continues down into town every 15 minutes or so," Maya replied. "It loads right over... right over...."

She looked around but couldn't see the loading zone because some tour buses from the big city had just pulled in, blocking the small sign at the tram station.

"Ah, it's right over there," she said.

"Thanks, miss," the visitor replied. "The kids don't want to miss the start of the 10 a.m. show so I'll have to get my first cup at the Ark. They may have forgotten the unicorns, but I know they haven't forgotten Star-bucks."

Maya shook her head, realizing one of the biggest problems in Noah's Town: the disconnect between its major attraction, the national retail-ers that had sprung up around it and the downtown core with its local-ly-owned, locally-focused retail mix.

Changing her initial plan, she hopped on the tram to the Ark instead of going to town first. She became a tourist in her own town.

Chapter 5

ALL ABOARD!

Maya took her place in the queue along with the others visiting the Ark. She had seen from the license plates in the parking lot that visitors came from far and wide to Noah's Town to see this amazing relic and to hear the story of the Great Flood.

Maya knew the story all too well, about how the town's founders came to this area aboard the Ark and how they believed it was an act of God that they not only made it through the Great Flood safely, but landed in such a beautiful place.

Originally, the Ark was left to return to the soil, its mission of saving civilization complete. But by some miracle, the Ark didn't experience any aging at all, at least that's what the ark-eologists said. With very little upkeep, it still looked much as it did when it landed here generations ago.

The deep scars from 40 horrific days and 40 nights at sea were clearly visible, even at a distance, but modern shipwrights who came to study the vessel said it was still seaworthy. They even bored core samples into the wood to see if there were any termites. They only found two, who obviously had not heard the initial call "All ashore that's going ashore" as the waters receded. Apparently they were traveling for pleasure not business.

Maya had forgotten how awe-inspiring the Ark was. While a lot of tourist attractions failed to live up to their reputation, this ship was formidable and magnificent. No wonder tourists came from near and far to see the Ark.

Maya bought her ticket and a cast member directed her to the entrance as he handed her a schedule of the day's events.

The first show would start in an hour. Part of the Ark had been converted to a theater where an experiential re-enactment of the Great Flood was performed three times a day. A lot of the town's residents were in the play, portraying both the human and animal passengers.

Maya took the escalator to the start of the Ark's interpretive area. She stepped off and right before her were Noah and his family, presented in a very Madame Tussaud fashion. Maya was startled how lifelike and familiar they were.

She jumped when Noah spoke to her. He and the others weren't wax, but real actors who told a Reader's Digest version of the Great Flood as portrayed in The Bible.

"Feel freeth to roameth the decks," Noah said as he finished his speech and reset for the next crowd waiting. "The play beginneth at 10."

Maya worked her way around the deck and then descended down to the next level and the next. Modern day cruise ships had nothing on the Ark. It was easy to get lost as she passed one stall after another, stalls that at one time were said to have saved two of every animal and living thing on Earth.

Maya got lost in time and place as she roamed the decks, looking at the interpretive exhibits. It was then that she heard the sound of a ram's horn, piped through the PA system. It broke the illusion, she thought, but it did let her know that the show was about to start.

Along with the other guests, she herded her way into the massive theater and took a seat. The lights dimmed and the story began to unfold, just as she had heard it told to her as a little girl.

The production was first class and the 40 days and 40 nights were neatly covered in under an hour and a half. As the audience wiped the rain mist from their faces, they rose to their feet to applaud the actors. Then the exit doors opened magically at once and the crowd dutifully flowed from the theater.

And there she saw another disconnect. There was no one outside to guide guests to Noah's Town. Visitors instead walked right into the gift shop so they could purchase their official Noah beards and stuffed animals that were on sale in a fitting buy-one, get-one pricing strategy.

The gift shop didn't even have a display of rack cards showing what else visitors could do while they were visiting Noah's Town. Visitors simply made their purchases and headed back to the parking lot.

Maya tagged along, catching the next tram. While most visitors returned to their cars, she crossed the lot and waited for the one that headed to town. It probably would have been easier to take her own car, but she really wanted the full tourist experience.

The tram pulled in about five minutes late. The driver looked as if he had just awoken from a nap. He seemed pretty disinterested in his job or in the few passengers boarding.

"Good afternoon." Maya said, greeting the driver.

"Yup, 'spose so," replied the driver, reaching over to the lever that closed the safety gates.

The drive into town came without another word from the driver. He didn't bother to welcome anyone aboard or point out anything of interest that may be going on in town today, even though Maya knew that the farmers' market was in full swing.

Maya did notice that the wayfinding sign at the edge of town had signs for the local fraternal organizations – the Elks, the Eagles, the Moose – but no directional signs telling visitors how to get to Main Street or even a parking lot. The Ark had made sure there was a big sign directing visitors to the entertainment complex, but the town had done little to direct visitors downtown or to other attractions.

The driver pulled the tram over at the only stop on Main Street.

As Maya got off the bus, she looked the driver in the eyes and said, "Thank you!"

His only response: "Yup."

There's some definite room for improvement in the tourist experience Maya noted. It would have been nice to feel welcomed to town and to at least have a sense of what there was to do once the passengers got there.

Maya made her way to the farmers' market, which was a favorite of hers. She loved that the farm-to-table movement had always been part of life here in Noah's Town. Visitors may have thought the town was trying to cash in on the idea, but the shifting desires of the public simply caught up to the town's traditional way of life.

It was fortunate that the Ark had come to rest in such a fertile place. The surrounding lands were ideal for a wide range of locally grown foods. Obviously, meat was not on the menu in Noah's Town, but the quantity and quality of the vegetables and fruits was such that no one thought twice about its logical absence.

The farmers' market was bustling by the time Maya arrived. A local band, Hoot & Howler were on stage, doing their tribute to Elton John. Everyone sang along to their rousing rendition of 'Crocodile Rock.'

Not far away, the various farmers were doing a brisk business. The crowd was mostly locals that Maya knew and a few tourists. "There's another missed opportunity," Maya thought. So many people were in town to visit the Ark entertainment complex, but few found their way into town. Her 'to do' list was getting really long.

Some things just never seem to change in a small town. For Maya, the market was a touchstone to her youth, when she and her parents operated a stall selling homemade ice cream. She and her friends spent a lot of time at the market, listening to music, helping out with sales, running errands and, of course, watching all the cocks, bucks, bulls, ganders and jacks strut their stuff, showing off for the girls.

"Nice, isn't it?"

"Yes it is, Mayor. But it's a little disheartening, too."

"Why would you say that, Maya?"

"I was just up at the Ark," Maya replied. "The place is packed with tourists. But when I look around here, there aren't the numbers there should be. People come to town to see the big attraction at the outskirts but only a small number come into town to enjoy the day, and even fewer seem to stay a night or two to explore what we have to offer."

"I'm not sure I share your opinion," the mayor replied. "The Ark brings in a lot of tax revenue to the town's coffers. One of the reasons why we were able to create your position is because gate receipts are up at the Ark."

"But we have so much more to offer," said Maya. "We live in such a beautiful place, with great hiking and other recreational activities. Our restaurants serve some of the best vegetarian and vegan fare in the entire country and we have some pretty unique shops along Main Street. But capturing those additional tourist dollars seems like a stretch. Maybe we're just too content with the status quo."

"Well, you know what they say, Maya. A bird in the hand is worth two in the bush."

Maya just stared blankly at Mayor Mare, trying to think of what to say.

"I think, Mayor, that sometimes it's better to kill two birds with one stone."

"Maya, I'm surprised at you," the mayor said. The Robins are right over there. They could have heard what you said. Remember, you work for the town now. I caution you to keep that in mind at all times."

With that the mayor galloped off.

"The day was not going well," Maya thought. Not only was there no connection between the town and its major attraction, customer service seemed to be lacking, and directions were non-directions, and now the mayor thought Maya was promoting violence against some of the town's fine feathered taxpayers.

She decided to cut her losses. After getting a bag of organic oats at the market she headed over to her office. She just couldn't wait until Monday to see if anyone had responded to her survey.

Maya snacked on her oats and logged into her account. She opened her email program, excited that there were 10 messages waiting for her.

Her excitement faded when she saw that it was just junk mail. Not a single reply to her survey.

"What is it going to take to get this community to take a good hard look at itself?" Maya said, exasperated.

"Tennith shoes," came the reply.

It was Vern.

35

"What are you doing here?" she said. "It's a Saturday."

"I could thay the thame to you, Maya. A busy beaver's work ith never done around here," he said.

"What do you mean by tennis shoes?" Maya asked.

"Thith ith a small town, Maya, not the big thity you lived in. Meet the people where they work and play. Pound the pavement, tho to speak, but not tho hard that I have to fix it."

Vern turned tail and left, chuckling at his little play on words.

"Maybe that was the only way to get information around here," Maya thought. They certainly aren't connected like they are in the big city. Or if they are, it's in a different way. Maybe pounding the pavement was the quickest way to get a lay of the land around here. Maybe Vern had a point.

Chapter 6

HOOFING IT

A new week presented itself and Maya decided that a new strategy was in order. If management by walking around worked for the corner suite of corporate America, then economic development by walking around the community should have its own merits.

Going the digital route was certainly not working as a strategy, so why not hear it right from the horse's mouth, or any other animal's mouth for that matter. She decided to go on a listening session and hear what businesses had to say.

Maya decided to make an impression around town. A lot of the residents and business owners knew her as an awkward teenager. Now she wanted them to know her as their local economic development specialist.

She donned her most professional attire and headed out the door. As she stepped out on the street, she stopped. In the excitement of looking professional, she had forgotten to forge a game plan.

But first, she had to start her day with her favorite latte. She was beginning to look forward to the daily messages printed on the cups. Today's said:

Nobody listens themselves out of a job.

Maya wondered how her coffee cup provided wisdom that was directed specifically to her each day.

"Well, I guess I will just start at the beginning," she said, turning north. "When the road stops, I'll start."

Main Street wasn't very long. After all, Noah's Town was a small town. Without the Ark, the community may have just become a ghost town as the animals and descendants of Noah moved on. But like many small towns in this world, it survived and thrived in a number of up and down cycles that rose and receded like the tide.

Like most small towns across the land, tourism was the main economic driver. As time went on, the businesses along Main Street evolved to reflect this. Sure, efforts had been made to diversify the economy over the years, but it was always an uphill battle. It was the old chicken and egg problem. Bigger employers needed a trained workforce, infrastructure and housing. Investors weren't going to build new housing without demand and infrastructure was an expensive undertaking for a town that depended on tourism.

The local business community couldn't bear the brunt of large investments in roads, sewers and new power stations. Thanks to the Ark, the town could easily handle basic government services and some bells and whistles, but it was at the mercy of tourism dollars and visitor spending habits. A downturn in the economy meant a corresponding downturn in tax revenue.

Maya remembered when a few major employers considered Noah's Town. There were times when the local business leaders believed that landing a big fish was the key to the town's future. The flirtations were often fast and furious, but eventually the company would run into a brick wall and look elsewhere.

Maya knew that it was a dangerous strategy to pursue. While no one is going to turn down a goose that would lay the golden economic egg, she knew all too well that a big employer could be a beast of burden sometimes. It was the old tail wagging the dog problem. More than one major employer has rolled into a town with promises of economic prosperity, only to become something of a spoiled child down the road, demanding more and more and threatening to move to another town if they didn't get their way.

Even large towns had suffered this fate. A major employer would close or relocate and the entire economy collapsed around it, because no one had taken the time to diversify the economy or better yet, invest in local businesses and entrepreneurs who would drive organic growth. A home-grown success is far more likely to stay as they grow as their community roots run deep.

Maya laughed as she came to her first stop along the way, Swannee's Souvenirs. Growing locally was her big strategy for Noah's Town. It was a long-term play, not a short-term game like a recruitment. But she knew that it offered the best chance for this town to grow its economy, that, and leveraging the Ark's draw as a tourism attraction and hopefully, a destination.

Swannee's was a perfect example. Swannee was a talented artist who made replicas of some of the artifacts that were aboard the Ark. Ark-eo-logists had authenticated these treasures, such as the bowls and eating utensils Noah's family used during the Great Flood. Swannee's reproductions were perfect in every way. What's more, she had created a second line of earthenware that was inspired by those aboard the Ark but were more colorful and artistic, geared toward the homeowner rather than the collector.

Her works flew off the shelves. She had recently expanded her shop and hired a few more artisans to help with production to keep up with demand. Now she was looking for the next logical step.

"I've finally caught up, Maya," she said. "But that next opportunity, I just don't know. I've talked to the folks at the Ark, but they have their own souvenir shop and operation. They aren't as nice as mine by any stretch, but the mass market strategy seems to be working for them, just as my originals are drawing the serious art and arktifact collector."

"Do you sell online?" Maya asked.

"I've thought about it," she said. "But I'm not sure about fulfillment, especially shipping overseas. That's a long flight, even for me. It seems like a big leap to take."

"I can see that," Maya replied. "Your work is exquisite. I think it would be popular in some international markets. I was thinking of hosting an exporting seminar and covering the process of exporting for local businesses. Is this something you'd be interested in?"

"Yes," Swannee shot back, honking in glee. "That and a class on e-commerce would be a big help."

"Does the local college teach e-commerce?" Maya asked. "Maybe I should touch base with the Dean of Instruction over there and see if we can offer something like that to business owners."

"I know they teach stuff like that during the day, but I have a business to run. Evenings or weekends would be ideal. I'm sure others would be interested in learning more about e-commerce and exporting."

"Thanks Swannee. I appreciate you taking the time to speak with me. I'll do some checking and see how we can get some education and training going around here. I think it would help you generate more income and reach a wider audience. I just love your stuff here. I know others will too!"

The day was already shaping up to be a good one. One down, several dozen more to go.

Maya thought for a moment about saving some time and making calls instead of house calls. But the time spent with Swannee showed her that it would take the personal touch to engage the local business community. It also gave her a better feel for what the town had to offer and what potential was out there to fuel some growth.

As she walked down Main Street, she started to make some notes about its appearance. One thing was immediately apparent. Store signs along the sidewalk were turned every which way. A visitor wouldn't even know they were in front of Al's until they walked by it. If they were on the other side of the road, they may have missed it altogether.

The sidewalks were also difficult to navigate. Lacking any meaningful zoning regulations, some of the shop owners used the sidewalks to display their wares. This created a traffic and safety hazard when sidewalks were crowded. The occasional crack in the pavement and lack of ramps at street corners didn't exactly promote safety or accessibility. There was also an obvious lack of public places for shoppers to gather and sit.

As she walked down the street, she came upon Paula. She was lurking expectantly over a parking meter that was about to expire, like a buzzard over road kill. As soon as the time expired she was writing the ticket, even though a tourist came dashing over to put more money in the meter.

"Well there's a real welcome to Noah's Town," she thought to herself, making another note. "Nothing like telling a visitor that it's time to leave."

Maya spent the rest of the morning visiting with local business owners. There were a few businesses that opened up to her and expressed their concerns and shared what did and didn't work. But, it was a hit and miss proposition. Some were too busy and asked her to come back; others were polite, some didn't see how she could help them. Others just had no interest in growing. But almost all of them appreciated her dropping by to listen.

Almost every business owner mentioned that no one from town hall had ever dropped by to talk to them except around election time. And even then, the candidate did most of the talking and made a lot of promises while the business owners just listened. As Tundra, owner of the popular Noah's Rain Globes shop, said, "Promises are like snowballs, easy to make but hard to keep."

"No matter," Maya thought, "all in good time." Getting even one business owner to be open to new ideas was a win and she was already ahead of the game, thanks to her visit with Swannee and a few others. Obviously, walking around was a far better strategy than waiting for the phone to ring or a survey to come back.

Maya headed back to her office after a bite to eat at Glenda's. As she entered, the office clerk held out a "While You Were Out..." message. "It's Vern," she said. "He's been calling all morning."

Maya wondered what was so important. Vern was always turning up at the strangest times, but was always too busy to talk. And now he was leaving messages.

On the third ring, Vern picked up the phone.

"Thith ith Vern," he said. "And who is thith?"

"It's Maya," she answered. "What can I do for you today Vern?"

"Oh, Maya. Glad you called. We need to talk. Do you have a moment today? Thay, two?"

"You got it, Vern," she replied. "See you at two."

Chapter 7

DAM IT!

If nothing else, Vern was prompt. He walked in right as the clock on the bell tower chimed the second stroke of the hour. Maya looked up from her paperwork as Vern took a seat.

He brought some coffee along, knowing that Maya had a weakness for a good latte. The slogan on her cup said:

A journey of a hundred miles starts with an argument over how to load the car.

Maya thought to herself how true that really was.

"It's nice to see you Vern," she began. "I know we've been meaning to sit down and have a chat. What can I do for you today?"

"I with it could be under better thircumstances," he whistled. "Every time I talk to the mayor about these things, she just cuth me off. She acth like I'm Chicken Little or thomething, and you know how the town reacted when the thky didn't fall. He wath a laughing thtock around here. Cocky Locky thtill won't let him live it down."

"I seem to remember that, Vern. But what does this have to do with you?"

"We have a problem around here and no one theems to want to talk about it."

"Well, I'm listening, Vern. Go ahead."

Vern went on to tell her about the flooding problem and how the town's wastewater systems were having problems handling all the water.

43

"I noticed that when I first got here, Vern. Main Street was flooded, but I just chalked it up to a freak rainstorm, the type we get here every once in a while."

"Thath the problem, Maya. They aren't just once in a while anymore. They are becoming more frequent and the town's infrastructure can't handle the volume of water we're getting these dayth."

"When did this start, Vern? I don't remember it being a problem growing up here. I mean, the street would fill with water now and then, but it always seem to drain away quickly. Has something changed?"

"The capathity ith still the thame," he said. "It's the frequenthy that's the problem. Look, I'm no weatherman. I don't make the water, I just manage where it goes and how it gets there."

"O.K. Vern, I hear you. You don't need to be short with me. Remember, I'm the new person here. I'm still learning. I can tell you that some of the businesses I visited today mentioned the drainage problem."

"It ith not a drainage problem, Maya. It ith a volume problem."

"Well, it is a drainage problem, Vern. We can't stop the rain. We just have to learn to handle it, right?"

"I gueth you're right, Maya. I didn't mean to be short with you. It ith just that the buck theems to be stopping at my deskth and no one is willing to talk about the problem for fear of scaring away the touriths."

"What's the solution, then Vern? Do we need to look at the infrastructure and see what we can do to increase capacity. I'm not sure how we go about these things, but I would imagine it's not a quick or inexpensive fix."

"Years, Maya," Vern replied, hopping down off his chair and turning tail. "We've been ignoring thith for a long time and no one wanth to lithen around here, except you. Thank you for your time. We'll chat again, thoon."

Vern left Maya's office and for the first time since she got there, she started to see the town she grew up in differently. It wasn't necessarily the happy little tourist town every visitor thought it was. Like any small town, it had its share of problems. The weather wasn't something anyone in town could fix, only prepare for.

Prepare for! That's something she and Vern could help with. If the flooding wasn't going to get better, the town could help citizens and businesses plan for it, weather it (to use a terrible pun), and get on with life in Noah's Town as quickly as possible after a major flood.

Maya dashed off a couple notes on her legal pad and headed out the door. While preparing for a disaster was now one of her top priorities, there were other things on her plate too, including visiting the Dean of Instruction up at the college.

As Maya drove up the hill to the college, she continued to roll around a process for getting this town ready for a major flooding event. After all, her notes about signage and over zealous parking enforcement didn't mean a thing if the town was inundated with water.

Vern had made it clear that these recent episodes weren't the last. The town's drainage and wastewater systems were straining to keep things manageable, but there would be a day when Vern couldn't work his magic, and no one knew for sure what a major flood would do to this town, its residents and its economy.

So many balls in the air to juggle. While the flooding issue needed attention, so did workforce, education and training. A town is really only as good as its educational system. The future is built on the shoulders of the next generation as much as the accomplishments of those who came before.

Maya parked her car in the lot next to the college and got out. She stood for a moment, looking at the stately building that had served the community dutifully, if not progressively, ever since the town was founded.

Dr. Orville Orson was the current Dean of Instruction at the college. He received his degree while going to night school, for he was something of a night owl. He was confident the college was serving the community's needs. All of the students were doing well and everywhere he went, he would see bumper stickers that boasted "My college student is on the honor roll."

This was a great source of pride, not only for Dr. Orson but also the parents who supported the college.

Sure, they had heard the horror stories about the state of education in other parts of the country, but Dr. Orson didn't really give a hoot about what was happening at other schools. He had a simple, unwavering philosophy, one that he reminded everyone of with a banner hanging in the gymnasium:

"Every teenager should get a college education – even if they already know everything."

Certainly, the parents of his students weren't concerned. The college was teaching students what they needed to know and they were certainly making the grade. Dr. Orson believed that college was merely a way station for all the animals in the town, a place to while away the hours before they took their rightful place in the profession their parents were in. There was little upward or even lateral mobility as each member of the community willingly followed in their parent's hoof steps without question.

There was a natural order to things. Parents would raise their offspring to take over their jobs when they were ready and then take care of their parents. Then, the next generation were raised to eventually succeed them in the economic treadmill that was Noah's Town.

Those who did buck the system, like Maya, went off to a big city college and rarely returned to Noah's Town. City life was a seductive mistress as new generations explored opportunities, met new people, discovered different cultures, engaged in intellectual conversations and even started their own businesses. Maya believed that her college experience matured her and prepared her for her future wherever that may be.

There would likely be more who were tempted to go to the city and get an education if it weren't for the fact that Noah's Town offered a comfortable, if predictable, life. Everyone just went about their business naturally. There were jobs to do and most townsfolk went about them without even giving it a second thought. Nothing really changed from year to year. Seasons would come and go, tourists would visit year in and year out, and the town's elders all had opinions, but rarely, if ever, acted upon any of them.

"Maya Morton? Is that you? I barely recognized you," said Dr. Orson. "Back from the big city, I hear. A rarity for sure. I was always disappointed that you didn't want to go into your family's business, but I hear you've come to give our local economy a little boost."

"That's a bit of a simplification, I think. I'm here to help the community grow sensibly, give businesses the tools they need to be profitable and expand, and hopefully, strengthen the community on many levels. And that's why I am here to see you."

"See me?" he said, his head spinning almost completely around. "What can I do for you, Miss Morton?"

Maya told him the story of Swannee and her need to learn more about e-commerce.

"E-commerce? Aren't sales good enough in her shop with all the tourists?" Dr. Orson replied. "Why does she need even more business than she has right now?"

Maya sat, stunned. After a long pause, she decided to take a different tack.

"Who am I to argue with local businesses?" she said with a smile. "But I think it might be prudent to add an evening class in e-commerce, just to see if there's any demand. I'm sure that our IT guy at town hall could teach it and if there isn't any demand, we can at least say we tried. No harm in that, right Dr. Orson?"

"Whooo said it would be a problem? We could use a little boost in our evening class enrollment. I never considered a class on e-commerce. Whooo would have guessed?"

"It'll be a hoot," Maya shot back, trying to inject a little humor, but Dr. Orson didn't seem to get the joke.

"Well, Miss Morton, thank you for coming in today. I must say that it's been a real joy to see one of our own go off to the big city and return to our little town. It can be refreshing to have new ideas from time to time. I must admit that even I can get into a rut now and then. You certainly talked me out of a tree on this one. Thank you!"

47

Maya almost skipped down the stairs of the college, finding it impossible to restrain the joy of making an impact in her community. It was a small victory true, but a victory nonetheless. Hopefully, some of the local businesses would flock to the new class so that they could expand their markets beyond the borders of Noah's Town. It was shaping up to be a great day.

And then the rain started. "Strange," Maya thought. It was pretty sunny when she walked into the college. There were a few stray clouds in the sky, but no threat of any kind.

The weather can be fickle in a town tucked away in the mountains. It reminded Maya of the joke everyone used to tell:

"How do you tell the weather in Noah's Town?"

"Look up in the sky every couple minutes."

The sky was definitely updating today's forecast. Maya made a mad dash to her car as the rain intensified, going from a drizzle to an energetic deluge in mere moments.

This was certainly going to put a damper on the day.

She was feeling a chill through her body and decided to stop at Al's to pick up a warm drink. She also felt she needed a dose of wisdom to go with her piping hot coffee.

The barista let her know her order was ready, "Maya, your salted caramel pumpkin latte is ready."

"Thank you," Maya said, as she grabbed the cup to warm her hands and then turned it to reveal the message:

People using umbrellas always seem to be under the weather.

As she made her way to her office, she could see the drains on Main Street straining to keep up with the pace of what had become a torrential downpour.

She grabbed her umbrella and timed her exit, extending the bumbershoot with a practiced flourish. A moment later, a gust of wind flipped it inside out, making it useless.

Increasingly drenched she struggled through the tempest and to the doors of the town hall, soggy from head to tail.

Well, there goes the day. Looks like I'm going to have to put off some of my appointments and start mapping out a crisis plan for the community, 'weather' they like it or not.

Maya smiled at the play on words as she made her way to her office. She phoned into her voicemail to collect her messages.

The first one was from Vern who wanted to let her know it was raining again, hard. Maya laughed to herself as drops continued to fall onto her desk from her mane. She shook her head, which showered Mayor Mare as she entered Maya's office.

"Uh-hum," the mayor mumbled. "I can see you already know that it's raining, again. This weather is turning our tourist season into a nightmare, Maya. The parking lots are nearly empty right now and the farmers' market had to close down for the day because several tents crumbled from the weight of the water on the roof. My favorite band, The Four Horsemen of the Apocalypse, almost got electrocuted on stage. And now Main Street is starting to flood. What are we going to do, Maya?"

"Open an umbrella factory?"

"I'm hardly amused," the mayor whinnied. "I need answers or the people of this town are going to be calling up the glue factory to see if they have an opening, if you get my meaning."

Maya got the meaning, loud and clear. Her mood had gone quickly from downright giddy to dour. After all, she wasn't some wizard who could just wave the weather away with a magic wand. She knew all too well what the realities of the situation were. No matter how everyone in the town wished it away, the rains were growing increasingly stronger in force and longer in duration.

Maya knew that any plan, no matter how large or how small, would need the support of the community.

That night, the town council met again. Small towns often meant small town politics and Noah's Town was no exception. The room and the players didn't look much different from the night she was named the town's Economic Development Director.

Willy was still going at it with the three owners of Straw, Bricks & Sticks, the local construction company, huffing and puffing about them being so pigheaded, which seemed obvious.

Councilman Paca told Willy to stop picking on the brothers and quit crying wolf.

The mayor called the meeting to order and gave Maya the floor.

"Miss Morton would like to offer her ideas for dealing with the rain," Mayor Mare said. "Let's all settle down so we can hear from our new Economic Development Director about how we can solve the issue."

Talk about being set up. Maya stepped up to the podium and took a deep breath.

"Good evening, everyone," she said tentatively. "I'm afraid the mayor gave me more power than I really have. I can't stop the rain. No one here can. Not even Vern. What we need is a plan. A plan so that we can prepare for the worst, as I think the worst is yet to come. A plan will empower us as a community, so that when the day comes and the water overwhelms us, we can protect our families and businesses, make sure our visitors are safe and kept informed, and prepare our community for the aftermath. As any firefighter will tell you; the first step in fighting a fire is knowing where the fire extinguishers are. Planning is essential to our success."

Charlie McCluck thought of jumping to his feet in agreement, but he chickened out at the last minute.

Though Mayor Mare was impressed with Maya's oratory skills – donkeys are known for that – she remained unmoved. The audience was on the mayor's side on this one.

Harry the hare stopped munching on his carrot and rose to say, "Mayor Mare. How long do we have to listen to this stubborn nonsense? How many times do we have to be reminded that we do have a plan, God's plan. It was good enough for our ancestors who weathered the Great Flood, so it should be good enough for us."

The crowd looked on in shock, largely because they didn't know hares could talk, as Harry had never really spoken up before and people just assumed it was because he was a hare, not because he chose not to say much.

The pig brothers were quick to chime in. "This is much ado about nothing. We build the best buildings in town and they can weather any storm Mother Nature can come up with. Spending all this time on planning will lead to a shelf of binders collecting dust, nothing more."

Maya interrupted. "I am not talking about just writing a plan. I am talking about implementing a plan, as well. After all, he who wants milk should never sit in the middle of a pasture waiting for the cow to back up to him."

"Well that is true," said Councilman Hereford, causing everyone in the audience to nod in agreement.

Al got up to speak up next. "Maya, I have to say, I think you're scaring the children in the room. What good can come from all this doomsday talk. You're beginning to sound like Vern."

Members of the Lurkey family gobbled the whole thing up, flapping their stubby wings in excitement. "The sky is falling, the sky is falling," they all said in unison.

"I agree with you Al," Mayor Mare said. "We've heard this all before. Maya is making hay about the whole thing, which is just making me hungry. She's been away in the big city for a time and doesn't understand the whole picture here yet, so everyone ease up on her. I say we all adjourn and take this up at our next meeting. Let's all go get something to eat, shall we?"

Maya knew that she was beating a dead horse. She grew silent, looked Mayor Mare in the eyes for the verbal whipping she just received before nearly everyone in town and turned tail.

The meeting adjourned and life returned to normal in Noah's Town. By morning, everyone had forgotten all about Maya's dire warnings. Peace returned to the town, as the rains of the day before gave way to sunshine. Merchants opened their doors to waiting tourists, children played games in the fields and everything went back to normal.

Except nothing was normal about the dangers the town faced. Sure, the sun was out again, just as it was before the sudden downpour. But the rains would come again another day, and perhaps not go away, as the children's nursery rhyme promised. Maya sat down at her desk, dejected.

"Time to go underground," a voice said. Maya looked over her desk.

"Hey there, Vern. They really cut me to the quick last night. Thanks for being there to support me," she said.

"Thorry, Maya," Vern replied. "It wasn't perthonal. I had to monitor the water levelth at the dam. We came pretty close to a real dithaster."

"I understand, Vern. No worries. I can fight my own battles. But getting this community to see what you and I see, I just don't know how we're going to do it."

"Ath I thaid. Time to go underground. Come on."

Maya followed Vern out the door and down the stairs.

"Underground? Where? I really need to figure out what we're going to do next here."

"You'll thee, you'll thee."

Maya had lived in Noah's Town all her life. She had to admit that she knew very little about what made the town tick. Like most residents, she thought she knew, but Vern was leading her into the bowels of the town underneath Main Street, down endless dark corridors, past rusty old pipes and wiring, dead ends and switch backs. This was the town's underbelly, a place few people ever saw.

Maya was glad she had Vern as her guide. "You could get lost forever down here," she thought to herself.

"People have become lotht down here," Vern said, as if he were reading her mind again. "But don't worry. I can find my way out of here blind-folded."

Vern greeted a couple of moles who were digging a new shaft under the town. He turned to Maya and said, "These are my ace in the mole for dealing with the problem near term."

"Even the mayor doesn't know what goes on down here," he said. "If she knew I had brought moles in to do this dirty work, she would kick the walls right out of town hall."

"She didn't authorize this work?"

"Nah!" Vern said. "I talked to her about the need to add more drainage under the threet and she gave me nothing but neigh-gativity. She was almost hoarse by the time I left her office, thaying we didn't have the money, we didn't have the need. She said I needed to shut my pie mole. But I knew better. Now you know better."

"Will it help with the flooding?"

"Not for years, Maya. You know moles. They move like thnails when it comes to thith kind of work. Turn them looth without a plan, like they've been utht to all these years and they are lightening quick. But as you've theen, all that lack of planning comths at a cotht. Tunnels go everywhere. Thome dead end. Others go nowhere. Thtill others make the problem worth, not better."

"So you have them actually following a plan this time."

"Yeth, my plan. I got tired of waiting for the town council to make a decision. Any decision. Tho I diverted thome funds from the parks maintenance and street cleaning budget to fund the new drainage tunnels. But ath you can thee, it ith thlow going."

Vern led Maya down a couple more long tunnels, turning here and there. Eventually, they came to a ladder.

"Ladieth firtht," he said.

Maya climbed the ladder and gingerly lifted the hatch. They were at the spillway of the dam, at least that was her best guess.

"Why didn't we just drive here?" she said.

Vern snickered and said, "What would be the fun of that? Bethides, I wanted to thow you what we're doing to improve drainage, even without the town'th help. Only you and I know about thith, Maya."

They headed into the dam through an access door and called up the elevator. Even within the thick walls, Maya could clearly hear the water rushing over the spillway, trying to pour as much water into the river as it could hold. It was a delicate balancing act, she thought. Too much water and you wash out the bridges, cutting off access to the town. Too little and the dam can't deal with the pressure. Eventually it will fail.

Vern pushed a button that was a couple levels up from the very bottom of the dam.

When the door of the elevator opened, Maya couldn't help but notice that the floor was covered with at least an inch of water.

"What's this Vern?" Are we in danger?"

"Not at the moment, Maya. But the floorth below uth? They're already full of water."

"Don't we have pumps for that?"

"Yeth. But they can't keep up. No dam is leak-proof and thith one ith no exception. The problem ith getting worth, I'm afraid. Much worth. We are doing the betht we can, but it's getting harder and harder to keep it all in balance."

"Is it going to fail?"

"I thure hope not," Vern said. "No, theriouthly, thith dam isn't different from any other in the country. It wath a depression-era project. Hundreds of out-of-work construction folkth built this. It hath stood the tetht of time. I am thure it will continue to hold. Ith just getting a little old, like me."

Vern continued the tour, showing Maya how the walls of the dam had some seepage in them. Eventually all this water found its way to the bottom of the dam. Some of it, the pumps handled. But the pumps weren't built to handle the volume that was required these days. And new pumps weren't in the city's budget.

"Does the mayor know about the pump situation?" Maya asked.

"Yeth, of courth. But mayors come and go and one kicks it down the road to the other. Pumpth aren't a thexy campaign issue like new jobs or new lights along Main Street. Infrahructure ith a 'thomeday we'll get to it' kind of thing. It's the old adage, 'if it ain't broken, don't fix it.' Hell would have to brake looth before we fix thomething that ain't totally broke."

Chapter 8

IT'S A DISASTER!

Maya awoke consumed with despair. She wondered if she had made the right choice to tackle this job straight out of college. Maybe this was the job for someone who was more savvy about small town politics.

As she stirred her latte, she considered the latest message on her cup.

> *The road not taken was not taken for a reason.*
> *Trust that you are right where you need to be.*

She began to think about her few brief weeks here. It seemed like it had already been years, given all the work that begged to be done. Still, she had met or become reacquainted with some wonderful people whose hearts were certainly in the right place. Yes, there was some rough and often unpredictable waters to navigate here, but the few victories she could claim seemed to make it all worthwhile.

There was so much to do still, but she couldn't dismiss Vern's dire warnings of impending doom. Yes, it was a little 'sky is falling', but the consequences of not doing anything was something she couldn't face. Crisis planning was something she never gave much thought to when she was in college or during her internship. Everything was moving the ball forward, not backwards.

Yet, that's exactly what could happen if the town failed to ignore the fact that their infrastructure was frozen in time while the town had grown up around it. The new businesses and public lands were great for commerce, but it also added layers on top of a system that was not built to handle both growth and changing weather patterns. And infrastructure was not a sexy election issue.

Trying to slow or even stop the growth of Noah's Town would have as big a chance of success as trying to slow or stop the rain. The die was cast in many respects, so the only option was to figure out how to prepare for a disaster and minimize the outfall.

A tall order, given the fact that it was natural for people to think times will always be good, there will always be business and tourists, and there was no reason to spend a lot of time planning for something that may never happen.

It was true the rains could return to their normal pattern tomorrow. The earth's weather patterns were so interwoven that a change in the Gulf Stream or the winds over the Sahara could set off a domino effect. Still, the science for climate change was solid, and Noah's Town wasn't immune to the far reaching effects of the industrial revolution and CO_2 emissions.

No one wanted to be branded a Chicken Little. His whole family had to move away from Noah's Town when the sky didn't end up falling. Too bad he didn't just say "the rain is falling, the rain is falling." He'd be right at least part of the time.

He'd certainly be right now. Still, it would be tough for Maya to sound the alarm. She was the new kid in town. The mayor and council would hardly be likely to listen to her doom and gloom scenarios.

Certainly, Zelda at the *Noah's Town Tribune* would have a field day. Maya could just see the headlines splashed across the front page in big black letters: "New economic developer rains on town's parade." It would be just like a zealous zebra to cast a poor light on a lowly donkey. She and her cub reporters would make a complete ass of Maya for sure.

Maya knew that whatever she did, she'd have to do it quietly. She needed to forge a plan that was a no-brainer, one that even the mayor and town council wouldn't poo-poo.

It was a big risk to take. Putting in the time required to develop a complete disaster plan would take up a lot of her already precious time. She'd have to do a lot of the work on her own time so she didn't run afoul of her bosses who still thought creating jobs was her primary role.

Thankfully, the day was fairly open for her. Her meeting with the mayor got canceled. She decided to see Charlie, for he would be the most likely to lend a sympathetic ear and be able to keep her plan under wraps.

As usual, Charlie was in his office at the incubator. Even though he said he was going to retire, he certainly didn't look like it would be any time soon. When she walked in he was on the phone with an entrepreneur pointing the way to some potential streams of funding.

"Maya, it's so nice to see you," he said, as he hung up the phone. "I've heard that you've been finding your way around town. I caught up with Dr. Orson a couple days ago and he said he had shared his idea for a new e-commerce night class at the college.

"His idea." Maya said, swallowing her pride. Maya should have known that he would take credit for the idea. After all, owls are natural predators and depend on other animals for food. So why shouldn't they also depend on others for ideas as well.

"Yes, we had a nice chat. Swannee had mentioned the need for a class like that. Dr. Orson and I had discussed what it would take to start an e-commerce course at the college.

"Glad to see you're already making a mark, Maya. I knew you would be an asset to this town."

Maya was glad to hear someone validate the work she was doing even if the idea was given credit elsewhere. One of the first things she learned as an economic developer is to let others take credit whether they deserved it or not.

"Charlie, I need your advice. Can I trust you with something?"

"Absolutely, Maya. I know so many secrets that I had to buy a new Samsonite collection just so I could carry them all with me."

"Well I hope it's their aluminum collection. You know what happened the last time someone bought leather luggage in this town. The Herefords were sure they were related."

Maya sat down across from Charlie and recounted the details of her tour with Vern. She spoke of the town's problems of handling runoff from random growth and the storms at the same time; and how she worried the town was teetering on the brink of an economic disaster.

"Well, Maya. I can't say I'm surprised. I've lived here all my life and I've never seen so much rain, and worse, flooding. This is a small town. I've heard from some of the business owners along Main Street who have had to deal with water seeping into their businesses, either from the overflowing drains or flat roofs that aren't able to hold tons of water without leaking. They just can't keep afloat, literally or financially."

"I don't really know where to start," Maya said. "I think we need to plan for the worst and hope for the best. But I'm not sure there's anyone interested in this but me and Vern. I can see it in their faces. Times are good. Business is brisk. Who wants to think about a day when all that could change?"

"It may never change, Maya. I'm talking about the attitude around here. I've fought it all my life. But just because I don't have the energy to fight the good fight any longer doesn't mean that the fight is pointless. Someone has to step up and speak the words no one wants to hear."

"I was thinking of going it alone on this one," Maya said. "I don't think the mayor or the town council want to hear my doom and gloom tale."

"Well, Maya. I think it's time to be a grown up. This is not only your job, but your chosen profession. Economic development isn't all about ribbon cuttings and jobs. Sometimes, the job requires you to help a community see itself for what it is. Remove the old rose-colored glasses as they say. Someone has to be a truth-teller."

"And if I fail in that?" Maya shot back. "Do I just find a new line of work? Or a new town with fewer problems?"

"There's no such place, Maya. Even Dorothy came to find that the Land of Oz was no paradise. It had its own problems. You're our Dorothy. You need to face the Wizard, call him, or in this case her, a humbug, and defeat that Wicked Witch of Water. You have the brains and the heart. Now all you need is the courage."

"That's a horrible analogy, Charlie. Pretty bird-brained if you ask me."

"Maya," he said with a laugh. "I can't tell if that was a dig or a compliment. Go face your demons. What's the worst that can happen? They laugh you out of the room and all this water kills the town and everyone in it. And if they do laugh you out of that room, you can still do that plan of yours on the sly. The world is made of plans that are never needed. But you have to ask those vexing questions, 'what if it is? And what if it works?'"

"Thanks, Charlie. You're right, of course. I owe it to this town to give them the truth. And I owe it to myself to have the courage to be the bearer of that truth."

Maya called the mayor and asked for a special town hall meeting, one that the public could attend. "Tell them that I want to address the elephant in the room," she said.

"Clem? What did Clem ever do to you?" Mayor Mare asked.

"I'll explain it all tonight."

As she hung up the phone, Maya wondered aloud, "Clem? Who's Clem?"

That night, Maya was ready to tell the truth about Noah's Town.

"Order, order," the mayor said as she started the meeting.

The room was packed, in part because a pachyderm took up half the seats. Many of the town's leaders as well as its residents had no idea why they had been called to a meeting.

"Maya, our new economic development expert, would like to address the elephant in the room."

"What did I do," the elephant asked. "I've never even met her."

So that was Clem, Noah's Town citizen that never forgets. Maya apologized to him for her poor choice of words. She then went on to explain the issues as she saw them: the increasing rain, the periodic flooding in the streets, the economic effect disasters had on tourism and the capacity problem that Vern had showed her, right down to the water in the base of the dam. She then went on to explain that while natural disasters captured headlines for a short period of time, the work of recovery and rebuilding was long term.

"She makes a very "relephant" point said Clem, showing off his linguistic skills. "It's affected our family. My son's carwash at the end of town is suffering. Who wants their car washed when it's raining all the time? Business is off substantially. He would be better off selling umbrella-phants. He even had to lay off some of the monkeys. And let me tell you, that was hardly a barrel of fun."

The room erupted in conversations between the town's residents. The mayor had to call the meeting back to order.

"Yes, tourism has been down as of late," Mayor Mare interjected. "We've seen this before, folks. Tourism is cyclical. They don't mind the rain. Maybe we just need a new marketing campaign with a catchy slogan. Something like, "Noah's Town: Where Lightning Does Strike Twice" or "Where Memories Come Flooding Back – Daily.

"We don't need a slogan, Mayor. We need a plan." Charlie stood up, and peered as best as he could around Clem who had hid his presence.

"Mayor," Charlie continued. "I've been part of this community a long time. I've been warning people for years that we needed to prepare for the day when everything wasn't all sunshine and lollipops. We don't need a catchy slogan. We need a plan. And we don't really have the luxury of time. We don't know if the next rainstorm will be the tipping point, the one that leads to a disaster around here. We're not just talking about dollars, we're talking about the livelihood of our residents, the safety of our visitors and the future of our offspring. What is it going to take to get this community to act instead of react? The clock is ticking and we haven't done diddly about figuring out what to do if things suddenly go south around here. We don't have a plan."

"We don't want to create a panic, Charlie," said the mayor. "We remember all too well the sky is falling episode. Notice that it's still up there, doing it's job... um, whatever the sky is supposed to do."

"Well, right now its raining down on us." Everyone looked at Maya. Her inner monologue had suddenly spilled from her head, over her lips and out of her mouth.

"I'm just telling the truth," she said, as the room fell silent. "Just ask Vern. He'll tell you."

"Finally, thomeone ith listhening to me," Vern said, standing up and wiggling his way past Clem. "I've been doing the readings every time the rain hath come and thingth are getting worth, not better. The exithting drain and wathewater thythtem can't keep up with the increathed rain. There ith nothing left to do but plan for the wortht and hope for the betht."

The council erupted into a bit of a hubbub as members mulled over Vern's assessment.

Finally, Council member Penny Guinn waddled up to the microphone and addressed the crowded room. As always, she was quite formal, her top hat and tails swaying rhythmically as she spoke.

"Uh-hum. My esteemed associates on the council are for once unanimous in their agreement that planning at this point would be a prudent exercise. As such, we are directing Vern and Maya to head a taskforce to study a plan for making a plan, in the unlikely event that we do indeed actually need a plan."

"I believe this meeting can now be adjourned," said the mayor. "The sticky buns Al brought are getting cold in the back. Remember, every dollar raised through sticky bun sales goes into our marketing fund so feel free to take several home with you as you leave."

Maya and Vern had their marching orders. All that was now left to do was the hard work that would hopefully save the town from a disaster of biblical proportions.

Chapter 9

YOU ASKED FOR IT!

The storm got worse as the night wore on. The waters filled Main Street, then worked their way down Second and then Third, inundating the parking lot to the point where the cars began to float away.

Maya could only watch in horror from the relative safety of the second floor. She heard the unheeded cries for help as the water rose higher and higher. Before long, she could feel the water touch her hooves. She felt the panic and the sense of impending doom as the waters continue to sweep around her.

She awoke, drenched in sweat. Thankfully, it was all just a dream. But even as she looked down on a dry Main Street, she couldn't shake the feeling that it could all come true. The weight of the world seemed to be upon her now that the council had tasked her with developing a disaster plan.

How could she stop a flood? Mother Nature could be a merciless taskmaster and there was really nothing anyone could do to stop water from going wherever it wanted to, short of Vern and his moles who were doing their best to keep the water draining away from the town, rather than into it.

Maya looked long and hard at the bustle of activity along Main Street as merchants readied for another day of business. The sun was now over the horizon and its warmth bathed Maya's room through the open windows. It was hard to imagine that anything horrible could happen to a town like this when the sun was out.

To the tourists, it still looked like some kind of paradise. Maya had once thought it was pretty charming as well, until Vern had taken her on the tour underneath the town and exposed its weaknesses and worse, its dangers.

Even if the town undertook a massive project like expanding capacity and diverting the water, it would take years. Maya knew all too well from studying economic development and crisis management that a disaster can strike a town at any time with no advance warning.

Even her morning cup was providing some wisdom:

It takes real planning to organize this kind of chaos.

While she couldn't stop a disaster from happening, she could do one of two things.

First, in some situations you can reduce the likelihood that a disaster would happen or reduce its impact. For example if the threat is a fire, one could conceivably eliminate any combustibles that are near a source of heat or get the wiring inspected to reduce the likelihood of a fire starting. If a fire were to start, one could make sure the smoke detectors and alarms are working, that there are adequate and well-marked exits and the fire extinguishers are fully charged and employees trained in their use.

Of course, a fire is just one of many disasters that can befall a business or an entire community. A good exercise for any business or community was to list all the possible crises that could happen, even the remote ones. This can range from the unexpected death of a CEO or a robbery of a business or a major natural or man-made disaster for a city, from the failure of a dam and collapse of a local mine to the sudden death of the mayor.

Every crisis has a likelihood of happening and a potential impact. The goal of any crisis planning exercise is to identify the impact of each potential event, plotting each out on a graph with four quadrants. The lower left quadrant are those events that had both a low probability of happening as well as a low impact (Green Zone). These were of little consequence and needed little to no attention. In the right lower quadrant are events that had a higher probability of happening, but still a low impact (Blue Zone). The goal with these is to reduce the possibility and not worry so much about the impact.

In the top left are the events that had a low probability of happening but a high impact (Yellow Zone). The crisis response then would be to re-duce the impact. And in the right quadrant are the events that had a high probability of happening and a high probability of being disruptive if not disastrous (Red Zone).

At some point, Maya would have the luxury of plotting all the potential crises that could occur in Noah's Town.

With limited time and resources, however, her immediate goal was to identify those things in the right upper quadrant (Red Zone). These have the highest likelihood of happening and the greatest impact. Proper plan-ning would either reduce the likelihood or impact, which would move it into one of the other zones, either ones with less likelihood of happening, less impact, or both.

Of course, with floodwaters, the only way to reduce the likelihood was to build more capacity in the storm and wastewater system or pray that it stops raining with such fierce conviction. She even considered sum-moning the praying mantis to assist, knowing that in Ancient Greece they were thought to have special powers. But while praying couldn't hurt, it wasn't going to move a Red Zone event into one of the other less harm-ful or less possible quadrants.

Though Vern was working on the capacity issue, that was a long term fix. The data was clear. It was raining more often and a greater volume of water was falling with each storm.

Maya knew that a Herculean task was before her. While she had done crisis planning exercises in a communications class in college, she had never really applied the theory to a real town, let alone a town where she knew nearly everyone.

"I'm too young for this," she thought. "I don't have the experience."

"Yes you do," a voice said.

It was Maya's father.

"I knocked, but you didn't answer. So I just let myself in. What's going on Maya?"

Maya recounted the recent events she had experienced.

"Now Maya, calm down. Your mother and I didn't raise a complete ass."

They both laughed at their family's inside joke.

"Your mother and I raised you to believe in yourself. As we've always taught you, you don't have to have all the answers. You only have to know where to look for the answers. There will always be others who are more wise or experienced than you at any point in your life. Use them. Ask for help. Two heads are always better than one, especially if you want to be in the circus."

Maya smiled. "Thanks Dad. You always know what to say, even if it's completely inappropriate. I mean, circus humor? Really?"

"You're the one that works in a circus, Maya. I warned you about a life in public service, didn't I?"

"Yes Dad, you did. But you also taught me about the importance of giving back to the community. I could have gone in a different direction, but I really believe that economic and community development are essential to creating really great places to live. You know, the old quality of place thing. I just never thought I would be tasked with saving a town, if indeed a town like Noah's Town can be saved from the wrath of Mother Nature."

"If anyone can do it, Maya, it's you. And remember, you're not alone. There are people in this town who care about it as much as you do. Maybe for other reasons, but they love it just the same because it's…"

"Home. I know," Maya said. "Thanks for the pep talk Dad. I guess I'd better get to work."

"Remember, Maya. You'll only fail if you fail to act. Your mother and I are very proud of you. We're your biggest fans and strongest supporters."

Maya thought about what her dad said. She knew she loved him when 'home' went from being a place to being a person.

Maya pulled a box out of the closet that she had brought with her from college. One by one she pulled out the dog-eared books from the box until she found the one she had been looking for.

"Professor Steven Fink," she said, opening the book to its opening pages. "So we meet again."

Professor Fink was one of the nation's leading experts on crisis management. He had literally written the book on preparing for and managing a crisis.

She took the class only to get enough credits in communications to graduate but was now glad she did. His textbook on the subject was nothing short of a graduate class in crisis planning.

Her recollection of the class began to invigorate her to take the action needed. The despair was gone, replaced by a sense of purpose. She may not be able to stop the rains but she could arm herself with knowledge to share with the town. Being prepared was not an economic development program; it was a way of life. After all, it wasn't raining when Noah built the Ark.

Maya packed the book into her bag and headed to the office. She knew that she could probably get more work done at home since she wouldn't have all the interruptions of life at town hall. Still, she was the new kid and she didn't want her absence to be seen as slacking off when indeed, this project was just the opposite. For the foreseeable future, crisis planning would be her life, day and night.

But first, a quick stop for another cup of coffee and wisdom.

Despair is most often the offspring of ill-preparedness.

Sometimes Maya just went to Al's for the inspiration and not for the coffee.

As she walked into her office, Vern was already there waiting for her. She was surprised to see him.

"Vern, I didn't expect to see you here," Maya said, as she set her pack on the desk.

"I thought we'd need to talk, Maya. I mean, we're in thith together tho to thpeak. Ith there anything I can do to help?"

"What do you know about crisis planning Vern?"

"Nothing, or next to it. But I do know where all the bodies are buried. I can give you a thense of whath pothible."

"I think that will be a big help, once I get my arms around this. I think we're going to need some additional help, too. Charlie would be good as well as someone from the Main Street Association and Farmers' Market to get their ideas and seek their support for any plan we come up with."

"And you may want to bend the ear of the folkth at the Ark," he said. "They have a vethted interetht in thith too, I would imagine."

"Great idea, Vern. We could definitely use the help."

Maya saw Vern out and then closed the door. She cleaned off the whiteboard in her office and started to map out the problem and the solution.

The problem, at least on the surface, was obvious. More water was falling on the town than the systems could handle. As with all complex problems, other factors were at play, including the natural terrain, the fateful decision of the town's founders to build in the valley rather than on higher ground, unplanned growth, and aging and neglected infrastructure.

As with most communities, Noah's Town was never really planned. It started small, just a few buildings cropping up here and there as the inhabitants of the Ark began to settle in the valley after the Great Flood. Homes followed almost immediately, then the first businesses, a few houses of worship and then dirt roads and finally streets to connect them all.

In some respects, Noah was the first economic developer after the flood. It was his job to not only go forth and multiply, but create an economy where all his offspring could thrive. Noah's Town was his first try at community building, but he forgot just one thing – a long-term plan. Growth from the start was haphazard.

As the town grew over the years, various officials tried to bring more order to development. Roads were occasionally realigned to move traffic more consistently through town as horses, then carriages, then cars became the transportation of choice. Electrification came along, as did the first sewage and wastewater systems, nothing more than hollowed out logs cut by Vern's ancestors. These eventually gave way to metal and then concrete pipes, and as they were added, electric lines were routed underneath the streets instead of being strung above, giving downtown a more modern, neat appearance.

And with all this progress came a new problem. As more and more rain fell, the utility vaults under the streets would begin to fill with water, creating fires and outages. Battered by rains that alternately saturated the streets then the ground underneath, the once smooth streets had begun to buckle and crack, slowing cars through town.

A minor inconvenience to tourists, but a potential disaster if the town ever had to be evacuated. The only way out of town was through the narrow valley, serviced by a single two lane bridge. It was fine for the amount of traffic that came in and out of Noah's Town every day, but in an emergency it could easily become clogged with traffic, or worse, completely impassible if the water in the river overwhelmed it.

Maya backed away from the whiteboard in dismay. Noah's Town, in a perfect storm, was a time bomb with only one way out and no scalable evacuation plan.

Worse, the community had no early warning system, no Office of Emergency Management, and no disaster plan, not even a basic one. Maya realized that this was all on her now. Preparation was definitely less costly than learning through tragedy. A crisis plan was only part of the solution. The town was going to need an emergency plan to save property and lives.

Maya thought back to what her dad had said. Obviously, others in the town had expertise and experience in working with emergencies.

"Of course," Maya said. "Clem would be a big help. In fact 5,000 pounds of help. Why didn't I think of asking him from the start? Time for a little walk to meet with the elephant in a room."

Clem was the town's Fire Chief. He also served as the town's only pumper, since he carried his own hose with him wherever he went. With a couple gulps of water, Clem could dowse nearly any fire within moments.

As usual, Clem was at the firehouse. He rarely strayed far from the station, just in case his services were needed. She was surprised he had been at the town meeting the other evening.

Maya knocked on the door of the firehouse. Clem was on the far side, shining some of the new nozzles he had just ordered.

"Maya, good to see you again," Clem said, as he lumbered over to the door. "What brings you to the fire station today?"

"As you may remember. Wait, what am I saying, an elephant never forgets, right?"

They both laughed even though she was sure Clem had heard that line a million times.

"An elephant never forgets but we are not mind readers", Clem clarified.

"Anyway, the mayor and council have tasked Vern and I with creating a disaster plan for the city to address the flooding problem. It's a tall order, Chief. I don't know where to start."

"Well, Maya. There's an old saying in firefighting. Fight what you can control and don't worry about what you can't control. In my line of work, that means decision trees."

Clem walked Maya over to the chalkboard on the wall. He deftly picked up a large piece of chalk and began making circles on the board, one on the far left, then two in the center, then four on the right.

"This is how we fight fires. It really works for everything, and bear in mind, this is greatly simplified. Now, say the first circle is the crisis we're facing. In my case a fire. There are two possible outcomes, which are the next two circles. In our example, the fire either is put out or it gets worse. We obviously want to put the fire out, so our next decision is how do we do that. That's the four other circles. We could spray foam on it, apply water instead, remove the fuel or remove the oxygen source. Either one of these may work. But which? That depends largely on what type of fire, how much it has already spread, where it is and if any lives are in danger. So we go back to the start with a new decision tree. Let's say there are lives at risk. So our first decision, in the first circle on the left, is that we are going to save those lives and worry about the structure and fire later. Again, we assess the situation and decide the best course of action based on the desired outcomes. In the real world, these decisions are all made on the fly, but mapping them out when we're not in the middle of a crisis helps us visualize different scenarios and walk through the results of our decisions without endangering lives or property."

"In your case, you can't stop the water from falling as you have no control over the weather," he continued. "But you can save lives by evacuating early. The question then becomes how and where. How are you going to get large numbers of people to safety and where is the best place to shelter them? Once people are safe, then you work on saving property, or at least reclaiming it from the waters once they recede."

"So we shouldn't put a lot of work into improving drainage?" Maya said. "Vern's been working diligently at that day and night."

"You should always be proactive in your planning," Clem said. "I spend a lot of time in schools teaching kids how to prevent fires in their homes. A lot of my job is education so that we can lower the risk that a fire will occur. Vern's work is just as important in this regard. But saving lives always comes first in our line of work. We can never stop fires from occurring no matter how much preparation and education we do. Fires are a fact of life, whether they are man-made or an act of Mother Nature. The only control we have is to reduce the chance a fire will occur in the first place and have a plan for fighting them if they do. So we do a lot of decision trees: If this happens, what do we do next and next and next. A good crisis plan considers all the possibilities and the desired outcomes. All the decisions made in between will spell the difference between success or failure in managing any crisis. It teaches you to think on your feet so that you can make decisions in the moment as conditions change."

"That's great advice, Chief. This makes everything so much more manageable."

"Just remember, Maya. All the planning in the world won't save anyone if the plan is too rigid. Your plan needs to be as flexible as a shark. There is a reason the dinosaur did not make it on the boat."

"No two fires are ever the same," Clem continued. "Make sure you build flexibility into every plan you create. Take the decision-making process out as far as you can and try to imagine all the variables. It's always the one possibility that you didn't consider that will trip you up. Planning for a crisis requires you to be smart, flexible and innovative. And remember, Maya, I'm here for you. Others are too. You don't have to go it alone. Your planning affects us all."

"Thanks, Chief. I really appreciate all the help."

Maya felt renewed energy to tackle a bona fide disaster plan for the town. Yes, it was a big undertaking, but she knew that all her work could not only save Noah's Town, but save lives, too.

As she stepped out on the street, the sun was shining and the town was packed with locals and visitors. It was another chamber of commerce kind of day and it briefly gave Maya hope that her plan would remain just that, a plan, one that would never have to be called into action.

Maya cracked Fink's book open as she ate her lunch. The pages were dog-eared, entire pages were lathered with yellow highlighter. Obviously, she had enjoyed the class.

While it would be easy to develop a disaster plan for all kinds of scenarios, Maya focused only on flooding and its potential consequences as they related to events that would unfold, both on the response side and the event side. This would allow her to develop response modules that could be mixed and matched to suit a specific stage of a potential flood event. This would also allow her to develop a plan that could be engaged early on, with the different responses spelled out in order, right down to activation protocols and chain of command. She could then use the flooding scenario as a pattern for working out responses to other crises identified by the grid exercise.

Planning was the key. During a crisis, winging it can be extremely dangerous and even catastrophic. A crisis, even a small one, required immediate, systematic responses to the situation as it unfolds. One of the keys to being ready would be regular drills, testing the plan in a mock exercise, seeing what worked and what didn't and what the city and emergency responders could do better the next time.

"Practice makes perfect in this game," Maya thought. She went back to her whiteboard to map out the first set of modules, the things that would happen within the first minutes, hours and days. Eventually she would assign officials and responders to these tasks, along with resources.

She would also need a Command Center, one that was in a safe place where flood waters wouldn't compromise communications or the decision-making process. She would need to see the Planning Department about that, since they would have the best sense of where the flood zones would be as well as potential spots to set up a Command Center when needed.

Maya was now deep in thought. She didn't even hear the mayor knock on her door.

"So, I see you've already been a busy girl, Maya. Clem told me about your little visit. I want you to remember that you still have other duties around here besides this crisis response thing. I would like a report on my desk at the beginning of next week outlining your work to date and priorities going forward."

"I thought this was my priority," Maya replied. "Isn't this what the town council asked Vern and I to do?"

"Yes, Maya. To a point. Notice that they didn't take anything off your plate; they only put more responsibility onto it. Taxpayers have a hard time understanding why we would be spending time and money on plans that may never be needed. Voters, I mean, residents, want to see job creation, more tourists in town, and maybe a new slogan. I love a good slogan, don't you?"

Maya could see where this was going. Disaster planning is never a priority in a town until a disaster strikes, and then it's too late. The secret to planning for a crisis is to be proactive, not reactive. That's what Clem said, too. After a disaster strikes, there's nothing you can do but react, which costs more in the long run than planning does.

But Maya didn't want to rock the boat, at least not yet. She bit her tongue, telling the mayor that she would have the report ready and on her desk Monday morning.

As the mayor left, Maya wasn't sure if the report request wasn't just a red herring and that the mayor was really just checking in on her to see if she was really up to this task – and perhaps even the job.

Chapter 10

MAKING PLANS

Maya's report must have made the mayor happy for she hadn't had another surprise visit for more than a week.

A good thing, since it gave Maya a lot of time to work on her disaster plan. Yes, other things needed to be attended to in the larger scope of economic development, but all this work would be for naught if the town found itself unprepared for a major disaster, or even a little crisis that would scare visitors away, close Main Street for more than a day or two, or disrupt supply lines or utilities.

Still, it was thankless work. Many in the town, from the chamber to the town council, would think this was make-work, work to fill space in a day or week when there was nothing better to do.

Crisis planning carries no glory. There's no award for a great plan that sits on a shelf collecting dust. The only true reward is seeing a crisis through to its logical conclusion, reducing the damage, minimizing the recovery time and saving lives.

Maya found herself in a bit of a funk again. Where was all this going anyway? It wasn't really what she signed up for, all this planning, endless decision trees and scenarios that may never even happen.

In the midst of Maya's pity party, she heard a loud clap of thunder. A torrential rain followed almost immediately and she started to laugh.

"Well, if that's not a sign from someone, I don't know what is," she said, looking up. "I get it, I get it."

She redoubled her efforts to get her first draft of the disaster manual done to share with the community and businesses. It would serve as a first re-al-world check with other members of the team who had provided input. Vern, Clem and Charlie had really been helpful. Now it was time to share it with other stakeholders, including the director of the Main Street Association, the Chamber of Commerce director, the manager of the Farmers' Market and the facilities manager at the Ark.

It would be the first true test. After all, disaster plans aren't written on stone tablets. They are meant to always be works in progress. Situations change, people change, conditions change. Responses need to change with them. An outdated plan is virtually useless in a time of crisis. As Clem said, knowing how to fight a fire is pointless if you don't know where the fire extinguishers are or if they are fully charged.

Maya went to the copier to crank out her first set of draft plans for review.

That's when she spotted the mayor. Mayor Mare was talking to her administrative assistant a short way down the hall. Maya tried to blend in with her surroundings, but that's pretty hard to do when you're a donkey.

"Maya," she heard from over her shoulder. "How is our little economic developer doing today?"

"Fine, Mayor. Keeping all the balls in the air around here. Jobs, new business opportunities, a new workshop or two, events for Global Entrepreneurship Week in November and a new Economic Gardening program."

"Well, that's good news," the Mayor whinnied. "We could use a community gardening program. The produce would be welcomed at the farmers' market. Buy Local and all that. Glad to see you're covering the bases."

Maya didn't have the heart to explain to the mayor that Economic Gardening was about creating an entrepreneurial approach to economic development, working with second-stage companies that seek to grow the local economy from within. The program provided these gazelle companies with assistance on issues such as core strategy, market dynamics and sales leads.

"Thankfully, nothing about the disaster plan," Maya mused. No condescending words of wisdom, as the mayor turned to leave.

And then she heard the clip clop of hooves, as they stopped, then turned.

"And our disaster plan? I know the council will want an update, since it was their idea to let you handle it."

"It's moving right along, Mayor Mare. I stopped sleeping and eating to get it all done."

"Good for you, Maya. Very smart. Maybe I should try that, too."

Maya headed off to her first meeting of the crisis crew at the firehouse. It was far easier to get everyone there rather than trying to pry Clem away from his fire station. Plus, there were only so many places in town that could handle the menagerie she had quietly assembled.

The meeting went better than she expected. Each member had a few edits and Clem and Vern both had some really insightful additions to the decision tree matrix and predictor scales. The team even assigned the various roles and Vern suggested that she speak with the Ark about the Command Center, since they had an old maintenance shed that wasn't being used at the moment and it was on high ground, overlooking the valley below.

Maya left feeling accomplished. Creating jobs and improving an economy are long-term plays. Often, it takes years to make substantive change in a community, but here in her hands was a solid piece of work, the town's first disaster plan, thanks to her insistence and hard work.

Of course, it was a team effort, but Maya still felt a sense of satisfaction about the work she had done. She only hoped it would never have to be put into practice for there was no situation in the matrix that wouldn't wreak havoc on the community she had loved since she was a little girl.

In some ways, planning for these disasters was pretty depressing. She knew the town had its share of problems, but the planning exercise had put them all down in stark black and white. Every dent and scrape in the community was now detailed in this thick binder. From a town planning perspective, it was a dark read. But from a disaster planning point of view, it was a potential lifesaver.

The team had discussed how the plan should be rolled out. Eventually the mayor and council would want to review it and give their blessing. But first, it had to be put to the test, so to speak.

A mock drill would need to be conducted to work out the kinks in the plan. While it all looked good on paper, a mock drill would surface any issues and create a more cohesive, actionable plan for the community.

Of course, blaring sirens and people scurrying about in emergency gear was hardly a smart thing to do in a tourist town. Acting out the plan as a full-blown drill would be disastrous, sending the community and visitors into a panic, a panic that would be real enough should a disaster actually happen, but not something you want to do on any sunny Saturday or Sunday.

Theoretically, a mock drill could wait until the off season. But Noah's Town really didn't have a down time. The Ark and downtown merchants made sure there were a steady stream of events, activities and celebrations to bring the tourists in. After all, it was the lifeblood of the town and the economic engine that drove its prosperity.

No matter. The real proof was to put the Command Center and its team through its paces in a realistic drill, working through various scenarios and reworking the responses over and over again so they reflected predicted realities. No plan is ever perfect. Plus, it will teach the team how to work together and how to problem solve on the fly, using decision trees and the rehearsals to make adjustments quickly, efficiently and accurately, with as much information as possible.

Roles were essential. Someone had to be in charge of the Command Center and there needed to be a strict chain of command to maintain order and streamline the response to any disaster.

Maya wasn't the one to be in charge. Her specialty was economic development with a little bit of communications know-how, not logistics or emergency response. Thankfully, the team selected Clem to be the Command Center Director since he was already chief of the fire department and had the most experience responding to a crisis.

Maya would serve as the Communications Manager, Charlie was put in charge of setting up the Command Center, including working with the folks at the Ark. Other members of the team assumed additional roles, from serving as the liaison to state and federal response teams to ensuring that the team had satellite phones and other technologies that could provide communications even if the power, cell towers, phones and other infrastructure were inoperable.

That was one of the things the team discovered as they worked through the plan for the second time. A scenario arose where the electrical grid failed because the cell service was overloaded by residents calling 911 and their families. Entire sections of the plan had to be rewritten so response mechanisms didn't rely on cell phones.

The team also identified a capital budget request which would include warning sirens, generators for the Command Center and other emergency response equipment, including the satellite phones that would be the life-blood of communications during a disaster. It might be their only lifeline to the outside world, and each other. Vern had reminded the team that the three pig brothers were ham radio operators who could provide additional support in a crisis. Maya made a note to follow up with them.

Being a small town, Maya decided that having a lot of computers, phones and other equipment stashed away in a Command Center was not a smart use of limited funds. The team decided the best use of municipal funds would be for the big ticket items that provided connectivity and communications. The team could bring the rest of it – laptops, phones, etc.— from their respective offices. That way everyone would have the system they were used to working on along with all the files they needed. They could just plug in, log on and be ready to go once the Command Center was powered up and online. Things wouldn't become outdated either, a definite bonus.

The Ark said it was fine to use the old maintenance shed for a Command Center. It was up to the team to furnish and supply it.

Vern said he had it all handled, which gave Maya a bit of a pause. Where is he going to get all the stuff we needed for a dozen or so team members, she wondered?

The next day Vern called to say it was all set up. Maya couldn't believe it.

"Come on up," he said. "I'll thow you around the place."

Maya's jaw dropped when she walked in. There were workstations and partitions, chairs and even a copier.

"Dam!! You've been a busy beaver, haven't you?" Maya said, taking in all the progress that had been made. She wasn't sure Vern took that as a compliment.

"I have. It helpth to have a couple moles to rely on."

"Where did you get…?"

"All the thtuff? The basement of town hall. The mayor wanted the whole place redecorated when she took office. The Naugahyde furnishings bothered her, I gueth."

They both laughed. "Her loss, our gain," Maya said. "Well, I guess we can have our first exercise this weekend. No time like the present, eh Vern?"

"Exactly," he said. "Thee you Thaturday morning."

Saturday came all too soon. As she drove up to the Ark, she wondered if they were ready. Then she found herself laughing. Like anyone is ready for a disaster, or planning for one, she thought. You have to start somewhere and as Glenda the Good Witch said, "It's always best to start at the beginning – and all you have to do is follow the Yellow Brick Road."

The road lay just behind the door beyond. Day One of the first official crisis plan for Noah's Town.

Maya stepped in, surprised to find the rest of the team was already there.

"You're late," Clem said sternly, before a smile came to his face. "We were all early, actually. I guess we're all excited. Shall we get started? I don't want to leave the assistant fire chief on his own for too long. He's such a baboon."

The first scenario is the most likely. Water is inundating the sewers and filling the reservoir behind the dam. The infrastructure is straining to keep up. Streets have begun to fill with water. Flooding is spotty, but widespread flooding is imminent.

"Folks, we are in emergency response mode," said Clem, matter-of-factly. "The Command Center is activated. Let's begin."

For the next three hours the team struggled through the exercise. There were obvious holes in the predicted response chain and at times, everyone simply ran into a dead end, especially when the flooding increased near the middle of the module and there started to be casualties and collateral damage.

Maya was exhausted. All that planning was for naught.

"Alright people, let's take a break," Clem finally said. "As I've learned in the firefighting biz, no plan is ever perfect. We have to come to terms that we may not be able to save everyone or everything. The goal here is to craft a plan and response that minimizes the loss of life followed by limiting the damage in order to get the town back on its feet as soon as possible after the crisis has passed. We may not be able to prevent the crisis and we will never be able to manage it with 100% certainty of outcomes. We need to stay on task, check our emotions at the door and do the best we can in what is at best a fluid situation filled with uncertainty. That is all we can expect from ourselves. After all, we're not human."

Everyone broke into laughter. Clem had lightened the mood with the human joke. If it weren't so funny it would be insulting.

The afternoon drill went much better. With the miscues of the morning still fresh in their minds, the team redoubled their efforts to think pro-actively, solving problems before they became critical and even staying a step ahead of the crisis at times, balancing the tendency to overreact, which often makes things worse, with the need to react systematically and deliberately.

"Well done," Clem said. "We still had a few blips, but overall, it went well. I think you've all learned that what is most important, especially in the beginning, is clear and concise information. This is not only important internally, but externally. We don't want to turn a molehill into a mountain."

"Or a mountain into a molehill," said Vern, looking over at the two moles working on the shortwave they had just installed.

"We'll meet here next Saturday to go through another exercise, building on the lessons learned here. Then we'll go to a monthly drill, if everything goes smoothly. As you all know, practice…"

"…makes perfect!" came the chorus from the room.

Chapter 11

NOTHING'S ROUTINE

Six months into it, the team was coming together. They were now comfortable with the Command Center's response mechanisms and systems. After a few hiccups, everything was up and running. The council had approved the small capital budget ask and had even supported the team to the point where the drills were moved from weekends to a weekday so various members of the town's staff could watch and learn.

For Maya, it was a small victory. She still had a lot on her plate and she worked long hours – often into the dark of night and even weekends – to balance her disaster planning duties with all her economic development work.

She had had some success there as well. Working with the college, she managed to get some night classes started, including one on e-commerce so local merchants could consider ways to expand sales beyond the borders of their community. She even offered to teach a course on marketing so entrepreneurs could learn valuable skills in promoting their new enterprises. Thankfully, that wouldn't happen for another quarter or so, but the wheels were now in motion to align workforce training with the needs of the community.

She even managed to get the mayor off her back after the gazelles told her that the Economic Gardening program she started was the best program they had ever been a part of. They thanked her profusely and bragged about the outcomes of their business' participation in Economic Gardening, not realizing she had no idea what they were talking about.

Dr. Orson had seen the wisdom of her work in connecting the college with the business community. This wasn't much of a surprise, given that he was, after all, an owl. But having his support opened some new doors and the college was enthusiastic about the new direction it was going, expanding its reach into the community and securing a new stream of students at the same time. The Chamber of Commerce even created a customer service class for all new employees of existing businesses. Dr. Orson was no longer "owl' by himself when it came to developing subject matter and teaching curriculum.

The work on Main Street was not going as well. On the surface, the business community seemed to get along with one another, but there were the inevitable territorial fights between retailers who were also competitors and it didn't help that some of the buildings along the street were actually owned by absentee landlords.

This wasn't unusual in a small community, Maya discovered. Investors in big cities often snatched up properties in smaller towns as a tax write-off. While landlords spent their winters in Florida, their property created an unsightly nuisance with overgrown grass and troublesome weeds. Fortunately, in the spirit of community-business philanthropy, the cows were great mooers and shakers and convinced the goats to trim the grass in the vacant lots.

There was a love/hate relationship in the minds of the retailers with those landlords. Rents were usually stable, but getting something updated or repaired was often an uphill battle. Often the shop owner ended up paying for the work after numerous unanswered calls to the landlord.

Thankfully, most of the landlords in Noah's Town kept up the appearances to make their stores visually welcoming to tourists. The town's maintenance department did a good job of contracting with the local businesses in keeping sidewalks in good repair. They allowed the Main Street Association to update things like the facades with a new coat of paint once in a while. Fresh coats of paint can do wonders for a downtown area, as well as planters and hanging baskets of fresh flowers. Based on their koala-fications, some Aussie bears were contracted to hang the baskets along Main Street. Plus their fur acted as a protective raincoat so they could work in the rain, which was becoming a real necessity for Noah's Town.

Clean streets and sidewalks were important too. Civic pride was obvious everywhere a visitor looked, even if some buildings had a few maintenance issues that were less obvious.

This was certainly true of the drainage problem. At one point, the town tried to create a Local Improvement District downtown, but the absentee owners made sure it failed, not wanting a tax increase to pay for improvements. The LID monies would have given the downtown area a new wastewater and sewage system that would reduce flooding and improve drainage. Owners knew it was necessary, but they didn't want to foot the bill. They thought the town should pay for such improvements.

Kicking the can down the road can be a dangerous game to play, especially when lives and property are on the line. In the last round of drills, Vern had added some calculations for worst-case water events, including one that projected future rain levels, based on the torrential rains the town had experienced of late. The system clearly could not handle all the water, especially since gravity plays a major role. While the rains downtown did not cause catastrophic floods on their own, the water cascading down the hillsides that surrounded the town eventually filled the aquifers and raised the groundwater to a critical level. In short, the water simply had nowhere to go but through town on its way to the river. Like a big sponge, the ground underneath the town could only hold so much water before it percolated to the surface.

The river, of course, had its own limitations. The dam was built in the late 1930s during the Depression, a project under the Roosevelt Administration. It was built to manage known water issues then, not now. The reservoir could hold more water, but the dam wasn't built to handle that much pressure. It would eventually fail, either partially or catastrophically. The pumps and spillway weren't built to move as much water the dam was now required to handle.

Similarly, the river could only hold so much water without overflowing its banks. In an effort to control flooding decades ago, the powers that be diverted the river and created levees, allowing more housing to be built on former flood plains. Development won out over common sense as the area continued to grow over the years.

Today, none of that land would have been developed. Modern zoning ordinances would have prevented it. But these properties were all grandfathered in and over time property owners had added additional bulkheads to improve the property value in a sale. These only added to the problem.

There had been times when the water rose right to the edge of the levees, but never over. Each time, the town took a collective sigh of relief as it dodged another bullet, falsely believing that it was the levees and flood control measures that prevented a calamity, not sheer luck.

Maya had become aware of all this during their many drills. Even though she had grown up here, she now saw the town in a different light. It was still a wonderful place to live, mind you, but the complacency of its leaders and a tendency to be cordial rather than transparent had taken some of the gleam away, at least in Maya's mind. She couldn't help but see the potential outfall of any major disaster striking the town, whether it was a wildfire spreading quickly down the hillside, cutting off escape routes, an earthquake that could cause a part of the mountain to give way, or a historic flood.

A flood. It was, after all, what brought about Noah's Town in the first place. The Ark was a daily reminder of the biblical cataclysm that led to the town's creation. And another flood, even a minor one, could cause such disruption and panic.

Economic development has always been a two-sided coin. With economic prosperity comes cause and effect. New developments create new problems. Old problems are often swept under the carpet or long forgotten. But they never truly go away. Eventually, aging or outdated infrastructure begins to remind you that growth isn't always a good thing.

While many economic developers want to land that ever elusive big fish – a major employer relocating – it too has its cause and effect. At times, it can become the tail that wags the dog, overwhelming a community with its demands. Then there are the communities that struggle to recover from the loss of a major employer. The heady days of economic vitality swept away in an instant. Living wage jobs that evaporated overnight, retailers experiencing a slow, then drastic reduction in receipts followed by the closure of shops and eventually downtowns that become ghost towns.

Maya had read the case studies from the International Economic Development's classes they offered. She knew that the smartest way to grow any economy is organically, helping small businesses grow into larger ones. Noah's Town had followed this strategy over the years. Not because of some grand master plan, but because they never had an economic development plan, or even a planner for that matter.

Tourism became the number one, and in some respects, only industry. In an ideal world, Noah's Town would have found ways to diversify a bit so that all its eggs were not in one basket.

But it didn't. Even though Mayor Mare thought Maya would be the one who delivered diversity, she knew all too well that it would take years, even decades, and that was if everything went perfectly.

Unfortunately, local economies are rarely perfect. A small business may eventually grow to be a big employer. Or not. Events may play out where the town becomes a destination for visitors, as with Noah's Town. A random event in the distant past sets the town on a course to be a tourist destination. Residents simply adapt to the conditions and occasionally seize on a new opportunity.

In other cases, a town experiences a boom-bust cycle when a rare or precious resource is discovered then depleted, leaving the town to thrive or die once industry has packed up and left. The history books are filled with communities with big dreams that were shattered by economic downturns, harsh business decisions or a lack of foresight on the part of the community leaders.

The same was true of diversity. Some towns, for better or worse, would become one hit wonders. Attempts to diversify were never successful. The town lived and died on a single industry or company.

In the case of Noah's Town, what would be a smart strategy for diversity? What would add value that wouldn't take away from the tourism trade? It was a delicate balancing act. Playing with the mix of local economy can be fraught with risks, even dangers. Even a seemingly small shift one way – through a change in zoning or the addition of a business that wasn't a good fit – could throw everything out of whack.

For Noah's Town, the die was cast long ago. The big fish in town was the Ark and the tourism economy it generated. With lots of nurturing and time, perhaps one of the newer businesses in town would grow organically, becoming a bigger employer than it was today. As Maya knew all too well, even a half dozen new jobs in a small town could create a shift in the community's economic fortunes, especially if they were living wage jobs.

Certainly this was the case in a tourism economy. Tourism wasn't necessarily a well paying industry. Many of the workers were at minimum wage and more than one had two or more jobs to make ends meet. Fortunately, the cost of living remained relatively flat in Noah's Town, as did the employment and housing situation. Demand and supply met one another somewhere in the middle, keeping costs affordable.

Pull tourists out of this equation and all hell would break loose economically. It did a few years back when conspiracy buffs began to spread word on the internet that the Ark was not the Ark.

There were sneaking suspicions that the idea was spread by the builder of that other ark, the one in Kentucky. That boondoggle cost Kentucky taxpayers $18 million in incentives and sensationalized the story of the Great Flood with gimmicks that included dinosaurs and unicorns as passengers aboard the real Ark.

The locals, of course, knew this was all hokum. Their ancestors had arrived on the Ark and the stories of the Great Flood had been passed down from generation to generation.

Still, tourism dropped for a time before the hubbub died down as other conspiracists turned their attention to the earth being flat instead.

Maya wished that theory was true, because then all this water falling out of the sky would just flow down the river, drain into the ocean and fall off into space as a cosmic waterfall, never to be seen again.

Maya couldn't shake the feeling that she was going to have to deal with a real crisis sooner than later. She just couldn't let it go, even though she had a full schedule that included appointments with existing businesses. In addition to those regular meetings, she also had a meeting with Dr. Orson about developing certification classes in vocational industries for a future workforce and with Charlie, working on his idea for a makerspace at the local library. She also was involved with the Chamber's effort to establish a co-working space for future entrepreneurs and a networking environment for high school students.

There was always more to do than time available as the town began to get used to the idea of having an economic developer who could help on any number of single issue fronts – from working with downtown merchants on parking issues and wayfinding strategies to working with town planners to fix a zoning problem.

It was interesting work and as every day passed, Maya felt more comfortable in her role. She'd even forgotten that it wasn't the opportunity she was originally seeking, that she had been railroaded into the position by the powers that be.

No matter. It was all hers now and she was making her way in her chosen profession.

She found satisfaction in the little victories. Economic development work was like the tortoise and the hare. Eventually she would be the famed tortoise in town, winning the race over the long run. But for the moment, it seemed everything else was passing her by as days ticked by one by one.

Fall was just around the corner and the days of endless sunshine with occasional showers would give way to cloudier days that offered the possibility of torrential, even epic downpours.

Maya used to love the fall. But now she faced it with a sense of dread.

It arrived suddenly in Noah's Town, as if a curtain had descended, closing one scene in a play and starting another. The days suddenly turned cold, the sky dark with rolling, boiling clouds.

The flora and fauna seemed to be the first to know fall had come to Noah's Town. As if overnight the leaves had turned colors and began to collect on the ground below and the squirrels were seen burrowing their acorns out of sight.

Maya changed into her boots and pulled a winter coat out of a still packed box. Her raincoat would be serviceable for the next few weeks, but she wanted to be ready just in case.

Perhaps it was all this crisis planning that changed the way she thought. There was a time not so many years ago that she didn't even own a winter coat, much less any coat. Now she found herself collecting her foul weather gear, locating the flashlight she had recently purchased and checking her kitchen to see if she had sufficient stockpiles of food and water.

Even though she had been schooled in disaster planning, her cupboards were mockingly bare. She had always meant to add sufficient stockpiles of the basics, but work had kept her so busy that she hadn't had the chance to properly shop.

That would be her first order of business for the day, one of her rare days off. Maya prepped a shopping list, adding items that were good for long-term storage. She also added batteries to the list since she noticed her new flashlight didn't come with them. And water, she thought. At least enough to refill the trough a time or two if the water supply was disrupted. It amused her that she needed water when all her planning was about having too much.

At the store, she saw Vern and Charlie. They were also doing their weekly shopping and picking up a little extra, just in case.

"We're going to thet off a panic, we three in the same thpace," Vern said. "Everyone will think we know thomething they don't."

It wasn't far from the truth. One of the downsides of being prepared is you can come across as a Chicken Little, like the sky is about to fall. And then nothing ever happens. Plus, there was the risk of buying too much of something and letting it just go to rot as the expiration dates come and go. Figuring out how to rotate stock in and out while keeping enough on hand to get through two or three days on your own is something of an art. There's a fine line between being prepared and looking like a hoarder.

Maya had it easy. She was just one person. Her parents had their own stockpile on hand, something they did without any prompting from her. Perhaps their own sense of preservation had motivated them. After all, donkeys weren't known for stockpiling food. That's something the bear family at the end of the road was famous for.

Maya was kind of envious of the bears. They would pig out in the fall, knowing that they would need all that extra weight to get through a long winter. Donkeys didn't have that luxury. Maya had to watch her figure, if for no other reason than she liked to maintain a healthy lifestyle.

None of that would matter in an emergency. All bets were off as survival became the watchword. Maya was deliberate in her shopping, making sure she stuck to her list, resisting the temptation to buy any comfort food that would just amount to empty calories.

As she trotted back to her home with her bags of supplies slung over her back, the rain began to fall. Maya picked up the pace a bit, knowing that she had left her coat at home. Harder and harder the rain fell. At last, she made it inside, shaking herself off at the porch as she entered her home.

"Wow, that came out of nowhere," she said. "That's some crazy weather."

She emptied her bags and put everything away. She could hear the rhythmic thumping of large drops pounding her roof. "It was like being in the Bahamas," she thought.

Maya had spent a few of her summers in the Bahamas. As with all tropical ports of call, the islands were treated to a late afternoon drenching most days as the heat and water collided in the skies above, creating epic thunderstorms. Maya enjoyed the storms, staying safe inside while hundreds of lightning strikes announced the coming of the torrent. She particularly enjoyed the smell of the air as the storm came to pass, the fresh ozone sweetening the tropical air.

A loud thunder clap over Noah's Town took her back to the islands, but just for a moment as she realized the rains were not letting up as they usually did, but rather gaining in intensity.

Maya was glad she chose to live downtown. She loved the fact that residential places were available in the historic Noah's downtown amongst all the retail businesses many of which were designed with an Ark motif. She could shop locally and her office was a short five minute walk from her home. In addition to living near retail, she was also close to other cultural and community attractions, like museums, the farmers' market, and parks. But downtown living did have its drawbacks in times of disaster.

She looked out the window to the street below. Passing cars of tourists heading for home threw up rooster tails of spray as they drove hurriedly down Main Street. Shoppers, unprepared for the rain, dodged the splashing water and puddles as they tried to get out of the sudden change in weather.

Maya turned on the television to the weather channel. Freddy was the town's meteorologist, and the local station's weather frog. He had grown up in a swamp right outside of town and loved the temperate rainy seasons of Noah's Town. Freddy had wanted to be a meteorologist ever since he was a tadpole. In fact, Al Croaker was Freddy's idol.

Most humans think the groundhog is the best predictor of the weather. But that was only a one day prediction. Freddy was a year round certified meteorologist.

If you've ever hung around a lake or marshland at night, that loud, high-pitched sound you're hearing is probably coming from frogs. And if the sounds of the frogs start to get louder and go on longer, that meant that a storm was coming. So even though the groundhog was peeved that he did not get the weather job at the local station, it was a good decision since Freddy did not hibernate like his competition for the job. Noah's Town needed a meteorologist they could count on all year round. That's one of the reasons why Clem also asked him to be a part of the Command Team.

Maya's phone rang. "I'll be right there," she said.

Maya grabbed her backpack, a bag of supplies she had not yet put away and she bounded down the stairs. She drove excitedly to the end of town, stopping at her office just long enough to grab her laptop and phone, just as they rehearsed. The Command Center had gone live.

Another drill, this one with special effects. Clem thought it would be the perfect time to conduct a more realistic drill. Freddy had predicted several inches of rain over the next 24 hours as a large low passed through the area. Winds of 30 to 40 mph were also expected, turning the event into a full-fledged storm. Nothing historic, mind you – it's hard to compare anything to the Great Flood – but a significant event just the same.

A gust of wind caught the door of the Command Center as Maya opened it. Charlie and Clem were already there throwing switches and getting the generator ready, just in case. The room was abuzz with activity, and as each member arrived to take their station, the mood was both calm and electric at the same time. After all, it was the first time the Command Center was active during a real event. While it was still a drill, the howl of the wind and the pounding rain on the roof made it seem far more realistic.

"Where's Vern?" Maya asked.

"I sent him out to survey the town," Clem said. "He and the moles are checking the drains, the wastewater system, and of course, the dam.

That's a lot of water for the infrastructure to handle and we need someone on the scene who can assess the situation."

"Won't the rain trigger the alarms," Maya asked.

"They will, but only when it's too late," Clem responded, looking up from his monitor which mirrored the controls at the dam. "We need an experienced eye to gauge things in real time, hopefully well before we ever hear an alarm. We want to stay ahead of the events, remember Maya? Sometimes the best way to do that is to have a set of eyes and ears on site, especially the eyes and ears of someone who knows the systems inside and out."

Maya knew that was a sound decision. She turned her attention to the local and regional news stations that were broadcasting radar images of the state. This was not just a weather report but headline news. Occasionally, a region would momentarily turn orange, then red as cells gained strength. The news was not good. The area surrounding Noah's Town was yellow with splatters of orange and orange-red.

Freddy, pointed to a spot on the map about 40 miles away. It had a hook on it, meaning there was rotation and even possibly a tornado.

"Everyone in the area, take shelter immediately," Freddy croaked. "The storm is heading northeast from the southwest at about 30 miles an hour."

"There's a possible tornado heading toward us?" Maya said.

"Surprise," Clem said. Freddy had left the station and was now reporting from the Command Center. He was briefing Clem and pointing out the projected path on a chart.

"People, this is no longer a drill. It is the real thing. We have a town filled with people with nowhere to go. They need to seek shelter immediately. Sound the sirens."

Charlie hit the button and the wail of sirens in a tower above the Command Center was almost deafening.

"Well, everyone had to hear that," she said. "I hope everyone heeds the warning."

Maya went back to her assignments as Clem and Freddy continued to track the possible tornado.

Thankfully, it disappeared from the screen 10 minutes later. The sirens sounded the all clear.

"That got the old blood flowing, right?" Charlie finally said. "I hope that's the worst of it."

"Don't count on it," Freddy said grimly. "The tornado was a warning that the air was highly unstable. Almost anything could happen at this point.

"Let's all stay focused people", Clem trumpeted. Freddy make sure you can report live. We want to maintain a direct line to broadcasters throughout this event. We need to be able to warn everyone if things take a turn for the worse."

Chapter 12

ALL HELL BREAKS LOOSE

Every storm has a pattern to it. Even a powerful hurricane flows and ebbs in intensity. All storms are driven by complex atmospheric conditions, influenced by countless variables such as low and high pressures, prevailing winds, tides, water temperature and the amount of moisture in the clouds.

This storm felt different from those in the recent past. True, the winds were not even gale force and the town had certainly seen far more rainfall, but this storm sounded angry, even vengeful.

With most storms, the mountains surrounding the town broke the storms apart, tempering their force and anger. But this storm seemed to find delight in weaving through the valleys, poking and prodding Noah's Town from all directions, as if it were looking for its weaknesses.

Birds can often sense a terrible storm coming days before it hits. Usually, birds will respond to drops in pressure and therefore seek shelter in bushes, in reeds, under eaves, and in nesting cavities before a storm hits.

But this was no ordinary storm.

Many birds of a feather started to leave the area. They closed up their shops, gathered their chicks, packed up their belongings, and headed south. Even the birds of prey recalled stories of how they lost brothers and sisters to unseasonal bad weather.

The residents of Noah's Town were surprised to see the birds packing up. They thought it unusual for them to be leaving so early to migrate south to find food. Little did they know that the birds were leaving because the atmospheric conditions told them to. This should have been a sign to everyone that something disastrous was about to happen. But, instead, that sign, like the hysterical Chicken Little, was ignored as the residents went about their business. "Fool me once, shame on you. Fool me twice, shame on me," the town would often say.

"This should have begun to break apart by now," Freddy pointed out to Clem in the Command Center. Historically, these things can't hold together like this."

Maya picked up her phone to call Vern. "No signal," she said. "It sounds like cell traffic is overloaded."

"Use the sat phone," Clem said. "We need to get an update from Vern."

Maya was just about to dial when the door flew open. It was Vern, dressed head to toe in foul weather gear.

"It's raining people outside," he said, knowing that the traditional reference to cats and dogs was a bit inappropriate since Jasper was in the room. He was a bit sensitive about being a mutt, with his papers still unclear.

"Vern!" Maya said. "I was just trying to call you to get an update."

"It's not good," Vern said.

It definitely wasn't. Initially shoppers simply went about their business figuring the storm would pass. Shopkeepers actually welcomed the rain for more customers came into their shops. It certainly benefited those stores that sold raincoats and umbrellas.

The rain seemed to make people hungry because Kneed To Know was filled with customers. People were enjoying the smells and tastes of fresh banana bread and other delicious baked items. Visitors opted to enjoy a bite to eat and a hot beverage, instead of fighting traffic leaving town. George was happy because his cash register had been ringing all day.

It was the calm before the storm to be sure.

A little boy was looking out the window while he chomped down on a peanut butter nutella coffee cake waiting for his mother to finish paying for his snack.

"Look mommy, the streets are like a swimming pool."

The mother turned around to find that water outside was rising almost as high as the little boy and climbing up the store's steps at an increasing rate.

Oh my goodness," she said. "There is no way we can make it to our car in this weather."

A commotion began as some people scurried away from the counter and towards the window.

George was curious what was capturing attention away from his banana and plum Danish with a coconut frosting. He left his cash register and pushed his way to the front of the store.

"Holy monkey feces," he said louder than he meant it to be.

The remaining customers also gathered around the window to witness water rising towards the door. They began shouting over each other. Babies started crying. Some customers became alarmed and stampeded out the door, only to return with their clothing soaked up to their knees.

"The water is rushing too fast. We could not make it to our car," said one customer.

George immediately shouted, "I will call town hall and see what is going on. I am sure this is only a short-term incident. We have the best engineers in the world in our water department and I am sure they are on top of this."

George was not sure that this was true but he certainly hoped it was. He had never seen flooding like this in Noah's Town

George attempted to restore calm in his store. "The water will recede shortly. But in the meantime, everyone can stay inside and we will keep you warm with the heat of our ovens, as my staff of a barrel of monkeys will be baking banana bread for everyone for free."

George was not sure how long the water would be rising but he was pretty nervous and tried not to show it. Monkeys are naturally afraid of water partly because they can't swim. The don't mind playing in the water but they avoid large bodies of water and this rising tide did not look like it would be going away anytime soon.

George and his troops of monkeys immediately started bringing out large sacks of flour for people to sit or lay down on. He did not want to start a macaque warning in his bakery and have people begin to panic.

Away from the sight of customers however, other shop owners were flooding 911 with calls, asking what to do. Emergency responders did their best to handle all the calls, but there were simply too many for such a small staff to handle.

The chief of police was already on the phone to the Command Center.

"What's the situation down there?" said Clem.

"It's ruff, real ruff," said the chief, a one-time veteran of the Special Forces K-9 unit. "I am trying to get some of my officers down there to assess the situation, but it's tough going."

The sirens sounded again. Few people knew what the siren patterns meant and it only created more panic.

There was a debate taking place at the Snooze You Lose Sports store. The hare was having his best day in business ever. He was almost totally sold out of rain gear and rubber boots. The hare was so excited to see all the customers in his store that he didn't even notice water rising through the front door.

However the tortoise certainly noticed as he began paddling to the exit.

"Should we close the shop?" the tortoise asked the hare. "What is that siren for?

Now, that is a hare-brained idea," the hare responded, ignoring the water at his feet. "Do you see all these customers? We are going to make a fortune. In fact, I am going to raise the prices on some of our waterproof items. Ka-ching ka-ching," he said rubbing his foot for luck.

"Rubbing a hare's foot is not a thing for luck. That's a rabbit whose feet have luck."

"Whatever," the hare replied. "No one knows the difference between a rabbit and a hare. It's like people don't know the difference between a turtle and a tortoise."

"I am a tortoise not a turtle," he said sighing in frustration.

The tortoise continued, "But sometimes making money may not be the most important thing to think about in times of disaster. What about the safety of our customers? We need to do something to protect them and to make sure they remember their visit to Noah's Town as a wonderful, yet exciting experience not a thunderous disaster in a town that abandoned them. We don't want them to tell stories of greed and that we took advantage of them by putting money ahead of their safety."

"What you call price gouging I call opportunity pricing"

"It's against the law," said the tortoise.

The tortoise turned around slowly in a huff. "I want to make sure my family will be safe so I need to start now. It will take me a half hour to make it to the car. And another half hour to get the wife and kids out of the house and into the car."

"Leave then," said the hare. "I'll handle the customers. You'll thank me later after the rains pass and you count the till."

"Better safe than sorry," the tortoise replied. "I'd rather live to see another day than make a couple extra bucks and go to jail."

"Oh, dear," the hare shot back. "It's not that bad."

Almost on cue with the tortoise's departure, a loud sharp crack was heard outside the store. People in the store gasped and looked outside. A huge electrical charge was seen in the sky followed by a long, low rumble.

Customers immediately dropped their store items and ran out of the store. Some even took their items with them without paying. The hare became frantic and was nearly stampeded. "See what you have done!" he said yelling at the tortoise.

"Me, what did I do?"

The hare got on all fours and started crying.

"Come on," said the tortoise inching towards the door to comfort the hare, "Let's get the shoppers safe, lock up and then check on our families."

At that moment, Bull Harris was patrolling the area in his 4x4 making his usual rounds when he spotted disturbances throughout the downtown area. The water was rising rapidly and was knee deep. People were stranded, babies were crying, children were holding on to their parents for dear life.

Bull stopped in front of Snooze You Lose Sports, "Harry, I am going to need all your lifeboats that are on your shelves."

"But Bull, those cost $99.99. I can't just give them to you."

The tortoise gave Harry a look that could kill.

Harry immediately reconsidered and said, "I will get them down from the shelves."

"I can't take everyone in the truck," he bellowed. "Give me the children first. Harry, pull those two rafts off the shelf and put them to use. We have no time."

With the help of a customer, Harry did as he was told and pulled the boxes down. He started to pull the handle to inflate them when Bull grabbed his hand.

"Outside, Harry, outside. We'll never get them through the door if you inflate them here."

Bull grabbed two more children and worked his way to the truck. Harry followed and took the rafts outside. The rains were stingingly fierce as Bull pulled the release handle. The first raft filled up almost instantaneously. Harry inflated the other raft while Bull tied them to the back of the truck.

"All right, everyone," he said, entering the store. "Single file, into the rafts we go."

Now, he was surrounded by water and the lifeboats became lifesavers. After dropping his first load to higher ground, Bull headed back again and again to rescue stranded residents and visitors along Main Street.

Once on safe ground, Bull ordered another officer to get the people out of town.

"Where should I take them?" the officer asked.

Bull called the Command Center over his radio. "Everyone is out of Main Street. Where are we taking evacuees? To the school?"

"Let's think about our options," said Clem. "The main road out of here is filled with cars as drivers are afraid to cross the bridge. And the spur road is below grade. If the waters top the banks of the levees that road will be a death trap. We need to get to high ground."

Other shop owners whose customers were not trapped inside and saw the torrential storms decided to close their shops as well. They flipped their open signs on their doors to closed and scampered away to check on their families.

What few of the shopkeepers knew was that the sirens sounded the alarm to begin Phase 1 for an evacuation of downtown. Because the sirens were so new, most of the residents didn't know what the different siren patterns meant and Zelda, the zebra weekly newspaper publisher, only ran a tiny story about it somewhere back on page 20 of the *Tribune* months ago. She didn't believe all this crisis planning and the Command Center was news. To her it was all there in black and white — total nonsense. She only put in the small article at the behest of Mayor Mare.

Large flocks of tourists started to leave at the sound of the first siren. Some of their cars were now stalled out on Main Street, for they misjudged the depth of the water. Other cars became stranded as they waited for the cars in front of them to move over to one side or the other.

Confusion preceded outright panic. The town lacked proper evacuation signage. The actual route out of town didn't take drivers down Main Street, but two blocks west on Third. It was on higher ground and was four lanes instead of two.

As Clem had mentioned, no plan is perfect and the 'to do' list was longer than the city had resources and money to cover. Signage was on that 'to do' list, but the crisis team felt the sirens were more important. If only they had done a better job of communicating what the various signals meant so locals and visitors would know what to do.

By now several officers had arrived downtown. They closed off Main Street with their cars and used bullhorns to communicate with panicked shoppers and shopkeepers as the waters continued to rise.

There was panic, but not complete chaos. Yet.

"The spur road. That's the old logging route, right?" said Maya. "It's a rough go as I remember."

"Yes," said Vern. "It's a narrow two-laner and below grade. If the river were to overflow the levees it would be inundated with water. The main road is above grade, so it should be fine, unless all hell breaks loose."

"Hell?" Clem said. "You mean?"

"Yes, if the dam can't handle the pressure, we'll have to dump the water somehow. The moles and I are 90% sure the dam will hold, but there's a lot of water up there after all the other rains we've had and we're not sure how much she can handle without opening all the spillways."

"That could be a disaster," said Charlie. "One of biblical proportions."

No one wanted to even imagine that as a possibility. The result of the last flood was sitting right next door.

Next door!

It was as if there was a collective mind meld in the room. The Ark was more than a tourist attraction. It was now a giant lifeboat. No one on the team had even floated the idea of using it during their many drills. Yet, it had weathered the worst storm in the history of mankind.

"Are you all thinking what I'm thinking?" Clem asked. "What's the capacity of the Ark?"

"The theater holds about 1,500," said Charlie. "The rest, I'm not sure since it's used for displays, storage, offices and shops. Maybe another two. I'm not sure its seaworthy anymore."

"Doesn't have to be," said Clem. "Charlie, can you check with the facilities manager? See if we can get updated numbers. Even the upper deck can come in handy, if need be."

"On it!" Charlie replied, grabbing his rain slicker as he dashed out the door.

"Maya. Can you get hold of the police chief? Get an update on the road situation."

"Already dialing," Maya replied.

"Vern. I need you to give me the numbers. I need to know how much water that dam is going to hold back until it is at capacity plus 10%. Also, I need one of your moles to head down to the river and check the water gauges. We may have to give up on going across the river."

The rain was falling harder, pounding the roof of the Command Center. Periodically, the rain would turn to hail, then back again and thunder struck the surrounding hillsides.

"Well, at least there's little chance of a fire right now," Clem said, trying to lighten the mood of the room.

The door opened and closed with a burst of the raging wind. It was Swannee.

"Downtown is inundated. It's like Swan Lake down there. My shop is three feet underwater. I had to fly the coop through the bathroom window. There was no other way out. The residents and tourists were panicking, trying to find high ground."

"We have some folks on it, Swannee," said Clem. "Bull is sending everyone to the Ark. Those that can't get out are being transported by his team. Can you sit over there with Maya and get on the phone to everyone you know."

Others took the cue and started going through their contact lists, creating a daisy chain of notifications to spread the word quickly. The pigs got on their ham radios and went to work. The Ark was to be the town's lifeboat and everyone turned their attention to getting the message out.

Maya was still on the line with the major news outlets telling them to announce that all residents and visitors should make their way in an orderly fashion to the Ark. Do not use the bridge or spur road as an evacuation route. Go to the Ark instead.

Charlie returned with the facilities manager from the Ark. Both were soaked to the bone, even though the Ark was right next door.

"All hell really is breaking loose out there," Charlie said.

"What's the status of the Ark?" Clem said.

The facilities manager was in a state of shock.

"The status man. What is the status?"

"She's dry and safe," he finally blurted. "Dry and safe."

"We need all the doors unlocked. How much food do you have inside? How many can you feed?"

"We had a couple of deliveries the day before yesterday," he replied. "So we can feed perhaps a thousand or two for a couple of days."

"That's not enough," Maya said. "We don't have enough food or potable water."

"The Ark is on a well," the facilities manager said. "We just need power to the pump."

"Route power from one of our generators," Clem ordered. "That should give us the water we need for these people."

The mayor finally arrived. "What are we doing here? The town is in chaos. Who's doing something about it?"

"Calm down, Mayor," Clem replied. "We are working the problem. We need leadership from you right now, not critiques."

"But I didn't have any part in this," she said. "I was the last person to believe we needed a disaster plan, let alone a Command Center."

"This isn't the time for blame, Mayor," Clem said, picking up the phone. "This is the time for solutions and right now I need to figure out how to get food up to the Ark in the middle of a historic rainstorm. Any ideas?"

"Wally at Food on the Run might be able to help," she said.

"Wally, right. Mayor, can you call him and see how much food he can get up here and how fast? The supermarket is a couple blocks away from Main but on higher ground. We need to get as much food out of there before the supermarket is flooded, too."

"Yes, Clem, I'll call him. But how? My cell isn't working?"

"Maya, get the mayor a sat phone and a seat. Welcome to the team, Mayor."

Maya had called her parents on the way to the Command Center but there was no answer. They were on high ground, thankfully, but they still needed to get to the Ark. The rain could cause mudslides and Maya worried that they would try to shelter in place rather than leave their home of 30 years.

There was little she could do now. She had a job to do. They all did. And no matter what personal losses they faced, they had to execute their disaster plan and save as many lives and as much property as they could.

Hours had stretched into a day. What started out as a harmless drill had turned into harsh reality. The rain was nonstop. Water levels continued to rise and the winds had picked up again. The emergency phone lines were not getting a steady tone as residents and visitors jammed the cell towers.

As the first evacuees arrived at the Ark, several trams headed back into town. The facilities manager had called in a few of his employees to help with the evacuation. Bull told them to focus initially on the elderly, children and those with mobility issues. Several scoutmasters helped direct the traffic into the Ark's parking lots to make sure that every space was filled. There was a steady stream of arrivals. Families poured from their vehicles, running for the Ark for shelter and safety, taking with them whatever supplies, valuables or memories they could carry from their homes and businesses.

The tourists were easy to spot. They carried nothing but the clothes on their back. They were totally dependent on the town to take care of them until other state or federal assistance arrived.

Clem had already been in contact with the governor and the head of the emergency response system at the state level. But they were still hours, even days away from providing significant response, especially since the only roads to the town had been cut off. Helicopters would be useless in this wind.

Those who evacuated early were the lucky ones. They made it across the bridge and could shelter with friends and family elsewhere.

The door burst open with a torrent of rain and wind.

It was Vern.

"There's no stopping it," he said. "The dam can't hold anymore. The spillways have opened to bleed off the excess water and relieve pressure. All we can do now is wait."

They didn't have to wait long. Now that other officers had taken over rescue operations downtown, Bull had headed to the bridge to try to direct an orderly evacuation there.

"Base, this is Bull," crackled the radio. "Traffic is backed up across the bridge. There's just too many cars for the road to handle. The bridge is holding, but the water is rising fast. People are afraid to cross it. I'm going to have to close the bridge and send everyone back. We can't afford to add that much weight with all the added pressure of the river pressing against it. It will give way and take everyone on it downstream."

"Close the bridge," said Clem. "Close it now."

The room went momentarily silent. Everyone realized the town was now officially cutoff from the rest of the world. There was no other way out. They were on their own.

"Maya, get me the Ark. She just became our lifeboat."

Until yesterday, the Ark had been Noah's Town economic savior. Now it would become a life saver. Those same decks that had housed the town's ancestors were filling with their great-great grandchildren, their children, and their children's children, along with tourists who were in town when the early rains turned into torrents, making evacuation impossible.

Thankfully, the worst of times often bring out the best in people. As the first residents arrived, they took up their makeshift posts at the Ark, greeting visitors, guiding them to various spaces in the Ark, clearing exhibits to create room for evacuees, making sure arrivals had something warm to drink and ensuring they were at least somewhat comfortable.

Two of the town's doctors, Drs. Doll and Phin, opened up a temporary infirmary in several of the Ark's cabins, taking care of any injuries. Swannee had joined them, given her nursing experience with Airborne units. Arguably one of the most altruistic animal species around, Drs. Doll and Phin helped out others in need, including possible predators and even humans. They adhered to the old adage of "treating others as you would like to be treated" and made no bones about going out of their way in caring for others.

106

Morris had managed to get most of the arktifacts out of the Mooseum before the waters flooded in. He stored them lovingly and carefully in the gift shop while being sure the arktifacts and replicas didn't get mixed together.

In the distance, everyone could hear small explosions. The electrical grid was giving way as the water filled transformer vaults under the streets. The town they all loved so much was drowning.

Nearer to the Ark, the sounds of sirens wailing could be heard over the roar of the wind. Several ambulances were arriving with the injured.

One of the first arrivals was Councilman Hereford. He initially thought the evacuation was udder nonsense and refused to leave. But a fir in front of his home had other ideas, snapping and caving in the roof, trapping him in his Lay-Z-Boy. He couldn't moove.

If it hadn't been for Willy he might have been dead meat. Willy happened to be driving by when he heard the loud crash of the tree. He dashed into the Hereford home to see if anyone was hurt. Beneath all the debris he could hear the councilman. He wasn't hurt too badly, but you couldn't tell by all the mooing and moaning he made as he was loaded into the ambulance. He was milking the situation for all it was worth.

Swannee was glad to see Councilman Hereford. They were neighbors. "So good to see you, Councilman," Swannee honked. "Now, let's see about that leg of yours."

In the Command Center the chaos unfolding outside was almost business as usual inside. All those drills had paid off. The command team was firing on all cylinders and some of its members even found time to catch a few winks in the break room, which had several cots for those who didn't sleep standing up.

The mayor looked exhausted. She had been learning a lot of hard lessons over the last 24 hours and looked beat.

"Get some sleep, Mayor," Clem finally said, as she nodded off in the corner. "You've earned your stripes today. Some rest will do you and the rest of us some good. We're not through this yet and when we do make it to the other side, you're going to need to lead us through the days to come as we recover and rebuild. There's a lot of work left to be done."

"You too, Maya. You need to get some sleep."

Maya started to protest when Clem stopped her. "That is an order young lady. Not knowing how long this will take we need to start thinking in terms of shifts. We all need to be at our best."

As Maya drifted off to sleep, exhausted, she started to dream about her parents. She saw them still in their home, safe and sound. They were seated by the fireplace, trying to keep warm now that the power had gone off. But at least they were safe and out of harms way. Suddenly a train rumbled by the home. But there were no tracks nearby, Maya mused in her dreamlike state. Suddenly, the wall caved in on her parents. The rain-soaked hillside far above the house gave way. Mud, rocks and debris filled the living room. Her parents disappeared from her sight.

Maya woke in a start. It was just a dream, but it felt so real. Maya had to find out what had happened to her parents. She felt as if the dream were a warning to her that they were in danger, or worse, became victims of the horrible storm.

"I need to leave," she told Clem. "I need to find my parents."

"Not in this weather you won't. You're not going anywhere. We are on lock down and I'm not going to compromise our operations to save as many as we can just so you can check on your parents. I don't have the resources to search for you and all the others out there who still have not found shelter in the Ark."

"But..." Maya implored.

"But nothing! See this list? This is the list of the missing and unaccounted for. Your parents are on this list. So are the parents of others here. And children and grandparents. I can't play favorites Maya. We are conducting a thorough search and rescue operation right now as the weather permits and you are an important part of this response team. You know this plan better than anyone else here and you need to go back to your station and do your job!"

Maya was taken aback by Clem's stern, almost cold response. But she couldn't argue with the logic. Still, she gave it one more try.

"Maya, I know you're scared," Clem said in a whisper, taking her aside.

"We are all scared. My son is still out there somewhere too, Maya. My son. But I still have a job to do. And I have to trust that God is watching out for my boy. And your parents. And everyone else out there caught in this storm. We have to hold out hope, Maya. Do you understand? Everyone needs you and I to be the beacon of hope in this hour of need."

Maya nodded, wiping the tears from her big brown eyes.

"I understand," Clem. "Please let me know as soon as you hear about your son."

"I will," Clem said. "Right after I let you know about your parents."

Maya returned to her communications post. By now the national press had caught wind of the crisis and was broadcasting updates. With no reporters on location, Maya took point, serving as their eyes and ears as the story unfolded.

A new report came in from the Ark. It was mostly good news. The Ark itself was still watertight. The number of evacuees arriving had gone from a steady stream to just a few. There were no casualties to report and the injuries were mostly minor. The additional food had arrived from the supermarket and the well was fully operational.

Maya checked the manifest of evacuees. She flipped through the pages on the clipboard and then looked up at Clem. She shook her head. Her parents and Clem's son were not on the Ark's list.

"Don't worry," Clem said. "They'll be all right, I'm sure of it. There are many still unaccounted for. Maybe they'll all be sitting in front of a roaring fireplace at your home playing a rousing game of Parcheesi. Knowing my son, he's blocked them with a couple of camels, just to make the game more interesting."

"I'm sure you're right, Clem."

Just then, the door swung open again. It was Clem's son.

"Peanut!"

"Dad, don't call me that. You know I hate that nickname."

"I'm so glad you're all right. Where have you been?"

"On a little errand," he said with a smile. "Dad, you know that a little rain isn't going to bother me. I mean, I run a carwash. A 36-hour rinse cycle doesn't seem like that big of a deal to me. It's more like an average work week."

"Errand," Clem said. "What errand?"

Let's just say I ran into some new friends."

Maya's parents squeezed around Clem's son.

"Mom! Dad!" brayed Maya. "You're safe!"

"Thanks to Peanut here," said her dad.

"Will people stop calling me that!?" Clem's son implored.

"He came to check on us. We would have been here sooner but he had us boxed in with a couple of camels."

"See?" Clem said.

"You were playing Parcheesi? In this weather?" Maya said.

"What else is there to do with the power out and the road blocked?"

"Blocked? How?"

"Huge mudslide, Maya. It barely missed the house. If it weren't for Clem's son we'd still be stranded there. He arrived shortly after the slide. He thought he'd check up on us. A little birdy told him we may need some help."

"Birdy?" Maya said. "Was it named Clem?"

"I didn't want to get your hopes up, Maya," Clem said, blushing. "It may have not turned out like it did."

"Rather than make our way through the storm, we decided to shelter in place and play a little Parcheesi. You know it's your father's favorite."

"Listen!" said one of the three pigs, oinking excitedly.

"To what?" the mayor said. "I don't hear anything."

"I think that's the point," said Clem. "The winds and rains have died down. I think the worst is over."

"That's why we decided to make our way into town," said Maya's mother. "From our vantage point we could see that the weather was clearing some in the distance, so rather than risk another mudslide that might take out the house, we decided to get while the going was still good."

"And you walked all the way here?" Maya said, amazed.

"Heck no," said her father. "We got a ride from the big guy."

They all laughed.

The team stepped out into the first rays of sunshine they'd seen in almost two days. The weather was indeed clearing, the storm had passed. At the Ark, the giant doors opened and the first evacuees emerged, two by two, down the gangway.

"Thank God for the Ark," Mayor Mare said. "Where would we have been without it?"

"Or a good crisis plan," said Clem. "We have Maya and Vern to thank for this. Without them, we would have been in serious trouble in this town."

"The town!" the mayor said. "What has become of it, I wonder?"

"We'll know soon enough," Maya said. "The important thing is we saved a lot of lives. We couldn't save everything, but we saved a lot of people today."

"Yes, I guess you're right," agreed the mayor. "The town is just a bunch of sticks and bricks."

"It's much more than that, Mayor," Maya replied. "It's the people that make this town. You saw that right here in the Command Center and in the Ark. We all came together to take care of one another and in the process, the town. True, a town can be repaired, buildings replaced. But you can't replace the people, for they are the town. It's the people that make Noah's Town what it is. Home. And I am so glad I came home."

"So are we, Maya. Just in time too," said Clem.

As a rainbow appeared over the valley, they all laughed. The worst was over, the best was yet to come.

EPILOGUE

As the storm passed and the waters receded, emergency responders from throughout the country descended on Noah's Town to provide additional assistance.

So did the media. Noah's Town was a media darling and front page news for the next few weeks. Parking lots were filled with news vans and microwave towers, all sharing the story of how a small town escaped what could have been a major disaster. The media highlighted how the business community came together to help people with their urgent needs of safety, food, water, and shelter. In addition, the town government was credited with being prepared to help business mitigate disaster interruption to enhance community economic recovery.

At the first town council meeting after the flood, the council took early action to begin the rebuilding process. The city brought in architects, planners, and other consultants who had experienced similar disasters to work with local businesses to generate discussion and gain input. They laid out a 7-point plan of action:

- Make schools and hospitals structurally and functionally resilient

- Require that utility providers identify the vulnerabilities in their systems and mitigate the deficiencies

- Improve the resilience of buildings to improve life safety

- Strengthen business continuity planning efforts by providing education, tools, and training

- Identify and improve signage for regional transportation networks

- Develop a disaster early warning system

- Hire a grant writer that will apply for funds to assist businesses and homeowners return to normalcy

Even Mayor Mare was able to say aye to approve this plan. It was the first unanimous resolution ever passed by the council.

As the plan was publicly announced, Mayor Mare made sure the media knew about it. She loved every minute of television time she could score. She was a natural in front of the camera. True to form, she took much of the credit for the outcome. A run at the governorship was definitely in her future.

Clem returned to his job as fire chief. He continued to run quarterly drills with the Command Center team, hoping there would never be another time it would have to be activated. As everyone on the team learned, a crisis wasn't a matter of if, but when. "Disaster preparation is relephant" he said to almost everyone he saw.

No lives were lost, thankfully. A miracle that was truly evident as you made your way downtown. Though there was no loss of life, the loss of property was substantial.

Most of the businesses along Main Street were in shambles. Some of the buildings would need to be razed, largely because they had been neglected by absentee owners for years and the raging flood waters and wind did what neglect alone could not accomplish, reducing them to rubble.

The mayor and the town council took a strategic look at the downtown and thought that this storm gave them an opportunity to think how best to rebuild the core of Noah's business district. With input from existing businesses, they made decisions for the long-term future of the downtown. Many of the businesses that were on the edge before the flood, did not rebuild. Instead they were replaced with public art and pocket parks for tourists. During the recovery period, the positive message to Noah's residents was that "if we lose our hope, that would be the real disaster".

The people of Noah's Town came together and improvised as best they could. For the near term, they would need to take care of one another rather than visitors. The storm not only left financial wounds but also emotional wounds. Many residents suffered a shock to their system.

Drs. Doll and Phin recognized that the fears, despair and disillusionment many residents suffered would require time to conquer. They immediately contacted the Substance Abuse and Mental Health Administration (SAMHSA) who provided Noah's Town with behavioral health resources that helped them recover from the storm. The doctors set up special clinics to help with the healing process. They also organized a workshop called, Health Impacts: Physical and Mental. The session covered distress symptoms, support systems and coping methods. So many resident registered that they had to move the session to the Ark.

Fortunately, the town was loaded with talent and a renewed entrepreneurial spirit after the flood. One of the abandoned buildings destroyed by the floods was turned into a co-working space that offered mentoring, networking and workshop opportunities for future entrepreneurs.

Several entrepreneurs discussed how difficult and chaotic communication was during and after the storm, especially with separated families. They used their technology skills to create an essential app to have on phones that would allow communication with family and friends in the event of another disaster.

A couple weeks after the storm Charlie officially retired, heading off to roost in the big city, which was a surprise to nearly everyone. Rumor had it that he had found himself a rich widow who bought him a fully restored Coup de Ville, his dream car, as a retirement gift.

Before Charlie left, he hatched a plan with Lionel, the SCORE director, to create a local investment fund for Noah's Town. As the former head of a lion's pride, Lionel had experience protecting and supporting others so helping entrepreneurs access capital was a natural. He understood that keeping funds local would facilitate much needed self-sufficiency and job growth in Noah's Town. The fund became known as the Local Investment Opportunity Network or LION. It's unclear whether he gave it that name on purpose to remind everyone who the king of the town was or just a coincidence. But, it wasn't long before many investors connected with entrepreneurs and saw their money at work in the community they loved.

And Maya? She still works in economic development. In Noah's Town, of course. She got plenty of attention from other communities and they were willing to pay a lot more than Noah's Town could. But she had come to love the town she grew up in all over again, even with its warts, and challenges, that was as endearing as it could be maddening. It was home after all. And it was definitely worth fighting for.

Despite her short time as economic development director, she had accomplished quite a bit as a result of the flooding. She established the Noah's Town Growth Fund that provided bridge financing until the Small Business Administration loans could be approved, and funded disaster related needs not fully covered by the SBA. She also developed a business retention program specifically for future disasters that included a national model for mitigation, preparedness, response, and recovery. She set a goal that 75% of the existing businesses would have a disaster plan within one year, but after one year 100% of the businesses had a plan in place. As a result of her experience and success, she even began teaching a disaster preparation and recovery class for economic developers for the International Economic Development Council.

The Ark continued to serve admirably as an emergency shelter for residents whose homes were damaged. They opened a small business center that assisted with damage assessments, as well as managing the Growth Fund and federal and state grants to help get businesses open quickly.

The town council was right there too, opening an office to help expedite permitting and waiving fees to get businesses back on their feet again. The local bank provided emergency loans to families who had lost everything in the flood.

For those businesses who were unable to return to their shops, the town provided a makerspace so that business owners could continue producing their products and selling them online. They even put them on the town's new economic development website that features local businesses.

Other businesses found a temporary home under the welcoming tents of the Farmers' Market, which expanded to accommodate them. This helped businesses like Three Bags Full get back to making money more quickly while Main Street buildings were cleaned and repaired. The Farmers' Market became a seven-days-a-week operation, catering initially to the locals, and then visitors as they started to return to visit the now world-famous Ark which survived not one flood, but two.

Not everyone was as fortunate to be able to take advantage of the recovery work and adjust to a "business as unusual" environment. Glenda's Golden Eggs restaurant was totally destroyed in the storm. After all, she was no spring gosling when she moved to Noah's Town and to start over would eggs-haust her. As a result, she packed up her eggs and went back to Canada where life was a bit more sunny side up.

Maya knew deep down that though the battle was over for now, there was so much still left to do. All the work that went into managing the crisis was nothing compared to what Maya and the town faced going forward.

The storm took 36 hours to destroy much of Noah's Town. Recovery, on the other hand, would take weeks, months and even years. Some businesses could open without the luxury of power or water and she helped them reopen as soon as they were able. It was important to give the community a sense of normalcy, even in a very abnormal period.

However many businesses and shops required the restoration of basic utility services. The town would need to find additional funding and animal-power to improve its drainage and wastewater systems.

It was often said that beavers do better work than the Corp of Engineers so Vern had his work cut out for him in an effort to restore the basic services. While the media highlighted the town's elected officials, Vern was hard at work as nature's chainsaw removing the debris from power lines and performing damage assessment in the affected areas.

In addition, Vern, one of the unsung heroes of reducing the storms damage with his clandestine underground work, sent out a national alert. And everyone in the animal world knows, once a beaver sends out an alarm, help follows. He tapped into the American Public Power Association Mutual Aid Network and dozens of utility experts donated their time and came to Noah's Town. Their work not only brought a faster recovery by increasing the size of the workforce, but also brought revenue to Noah's Town hotels and restaurants. For his work, Vern was awarded the Public Employee Citizen of the Year, a healthy raise, an increased budget, and a year's supply of twigs, foliage, bark, and aquatic plants.

The town council also needed to look at building codes to ensure that any new buildings would survive a major rain and wind event. They passed a resolution requiring disclosures of disaster hazards in real estate transactions.

This, of course, made the owners of Straw, Sticks and Bricks squeal with glee. Not to sound piggish, but they saw nothing but dollar signs as their business shifted to handle all the remodels and new constructions around town. They even brought a new business partner aboard, Willy. Pigs and a wolf bringing home the bacon together. Who in Noah's Town would have believed that before the storm?

Maya worked side by side with the businesses throughout the recovery stage. She recognized that volunteerism in Noah's Town was the cornerstone to a healthy community. As the floodwaters receded, she helped organize community clean up teams to remove debris from the business district. Many businesses provided paid time off for employees to volunteer helping their business neighbors.

Dr. Orson from the community college stepped up to work with Maya and the business community to design classes and offer degrees and certifications in emergency management that became nationally recognized. The certification provided a variety of professions for students to consider. The storm also created opportunities as classes were created that taught retrofitting to engineers who inspect and oversee building development.

Even the hospital required their staff to attend regular classes on hospital preparedness. Health care providers were taught to prepare for and respond to the needs of victims of natural or man-made disasters.

Shortly after the storm, Morris began interviewing the residents of Noah's Town describing their harrowing adventures and their road to recovery. He felt not only that it was a story to be preserved for the next generation like the original Ark experience, but also it was a part of safety education. He enhanced his story telling to compliment the arktifacts he had collected at the Mooseum. He even started teaching the art of story telling at the college and wrote a book on the storm, *Noah's Ark 2.0*. It became a best seller and got him his own show on Animal Planet.

And finally there was Al Capachino, the wise and prescient coffeemaker. He continued to make coffee and dispense words of wisdom like a Chinese fortune cookie that made Noah's residents feel good about themselves and the future.

As Maya strolled to her office, sipping her double tall latte skinny, no foam, she smiled as she silently read:

When disaster strikes, the time to prepare has passed.

Roles of an Economic Developer*

NORMAL ROLES	**ROLES IN A DISASTER** *above normal roles*
Understands strengths, weaknesses and comparative advantages of local economy and local business climate. Provides quantitative and qualitative information to decision makers.	*Before a Disaster:* Seeks to understand vulnerabilities and risks to critical industries and businesses within the community
Develops programs to support business retention and new investment. Tracks the business community's health and vitality. Keeps public officials and the general public adequately informed on costs and benefits of economic development initiatives.	*After a Disaster:* Develops and distributes a disaster business recovery guide and addresses physical damage and business interruption impacts to industries and businesses. Facilitates the communication of accurate response and recovery information between local businesses and local government and communicates dual messages.
Acts as visionary leader who peers over the economic horizon to see what partnerships (both public and private) can be formed to stimulate working relationships in the future. Engages key stakeholders in visioning process to identify goals, strategies and resources for economic development.	*Before a Disaster:* Establishes an economic recovery group to identify immediate and long-term recovery resources and strategies. After a Disaster: Envisions how the community can build back to be stronger and more resilient.

Provides incentives to leverage the investment or involvement of different public and private sectors.

After a Disaster: Creates a strategic plan for economic recovery embraced by the community.

Acts as a catalyst and connector who invokes enthusiasm and excitement for projects that can bring positive change to a community's future.

After a Disaster: Connects public-private resources for building back better.

Provides assistance where the private sector cannot or will not meet community and business needs.

After a Disaster: Conducts concerted BRE outreach to reconnect with businesses and identify at risk companies.

Leverages financing to facilitate enterprise development, assists existing businesses with expansion and works to attract new businesses.

After a Disaster: Assists with short term and long term financing and business counseling, particularly for small and at-risk businesses and develops programs to support long-term recovery.

---

* *Master Your Disaster: Your Readiness, Response, and Recovery Guide*, Leanne Hackman-Carty and http://restoreyoureconomy.org.

Business Continuity Checklist

Pre-planning will help get a business up to speed more quickly once a crisis happens. Below is a summary of a crisis business plan from *When Trouble Strikes: A Crisis Planner.* Go to choosewashingtonstate.com/media-center/publications for more complete business checklist guidance.

ADVANCE PLANNING CHECKLIST

1. Identify a Continuity Operations team for your company.
2. Decide who can order a reduction, shutdown or relocation of operations in times of crisis or immediately following a crisis.
3. Create duplicate records of all critical business documents.
4. Back up all key data on servers and company computers to the cloud or remote server locations.
5. Identify all the functions that are critical to survival. These are the services that need to be maintained during a crisis and/or restored following a crisis.
6. Develop and maintain a technology plan
7. Develop a plan to continue payroll, billing and collection functions.
8. Alternate locations to continue office, customer and fulfillment needs.

IF A REDUCTION, SHUTDOWN OR RELOCATION IS POSSIBLE

1. Inform the president/owner and contact the CCC Manager.
2. Follow the instructions in the Business Continuity Plan and the Crisis Communications Plan for the specific incident in question.
3. Notify personnel, board, customers and suppliers of the potential for a slowdown, shutdown or relocation.
4. Test the employee section of your website and out-of-town phone number employees can contact to leave an 'ok message' in a crisis.

IF A REDUCTION, SHUTDOWN OR RELOCATION IS REQUIRED
1. Activate the Continuity Plan and the Crisis Communications Plan.
2. Secure the company's facilities as outlined in each plan.
3. Notify stakeholders. Give them further instructions.
4. Determine near-term liquidity needs.
5. Arrange for mail to be stopped, held or forwarded temporarily.
6. Track the recovery expenses of all personnel for possible reimbursement, such as overtime, travel or equipment rentals.
7. Record any injuries in the OSHA logs and be sure you report these to the state's L&I department.
8. Determine what resources (staff, technology, equipment, facilities, etc.) are needed to move back, reopen or restart operations.
9. Create a phased approach to resume full operations.
10. Communicate this plan to the Business Continuity Plan team, president/owner and CCC Manager.
11. Communicate this plan to employees.

REOPENING OPERATIONS
1. Inspect facilities for damage. Get necessary state, county and local approvals to return to operations.
2. Confirm with local authorities that it is safe for employees to return to work (i.e., roads are clear, bridges are safe, etc.).
3. Re-establish utilities.
4. Establish business priorities.
5. Contact initial staffing needed to reopen for business.
6. Inventory damages.
7. Check documentation requirements for insurance, federal, state and local disaster aid, etc.
8. Re-establish computer systems, retrieve back ups.
9. Contact vendors.
10. Bring in all services that were performed remotely.
11. Bring personnel back in phases to support functions as they are restored.

Resources

There are literally thousands of publications and websites available to communities to assist in disaster and recovery preparation. These are just a few of the resources that can assist with your response needs.

ORGANIZATIONS

- Red Cross

- Federal Emergency Management Agency (FEMA)

- DisasterAssistance.gov

- Small Business Administration: www.sba.gov/disaster-assistance

- International Sustainable Resilience Center https://ippprc.org

- International Medical Corps

- Direct Relief: www.directrelief.org

BOOKS, REPORTS AND GUIDES

Master Your Disaster: Your Readiness, Response, and Recovery Guide by Leanne Hackman-Carty

The Disaster Recovery Handbook: A Step by Step Plan to Ensure Business Continuity and Protect Vital Operations by Michael Wallace

*Prepare for the Worst, Plan for the Best: Disaster Preparedness and Recovery for Small Businesse*s by Donna R. Childs

Long Term Community Recovery Planning Process: A Self-Help Guide by FEMA (free online)

When Trouble Strikes: A Crisis Planner for Businesses Washington State Department of Commerce (free online)

Measuring the State of Disaster Philanthropy by Center for Disaster Philanthropy www.issuelab.org/resources/33250/33250.pdf

Crisis Management: Planning for the Inevitable by Steven Fink

TOOLKITS

Saskatchewan Economic Disaster Recovery Toolkit
www.saskeconomicrecovery.com

Community Recovery Management Toolkit
www.fema.gov/community-recovery-management-toolkit

Leadership in Times of Crisis: A Toolkit for Economic Recovery and Resiliency by International Economic Development Council

Community Toolkit for Economic Recovery and Resiliency (Canadian Version)

WEBSITES

RestoreYourEconomy.org
A one-stop shop for disaster preparedness, post-disaster economic recovery, and disaster resiliency resources, tools, event announcements as well as opportunities to connect with peers through social media groups.

US Food and Drug Administration
Provides steps you can take to preserve your food and water during storms.

SCORE
Offers a variety of free resources to help your business prepare for natural disasters and build a more resilient community. Includes numerous checklists by disaster and a small business planning guide.

FEMA www.fema.gov
Provides information where survivors may go for information about their programs and help survivors apply for federal disaster assistance.

Disaster Assistance
www.disasterassistance.gov
Provides numerous resources and a search tool that searches multiple websites to for the appropriate disaster resources.

Crowd Source Rescue
https://crowdsourcerescue.com
Connect people who need help during a crisis with local volunteers.

Hurricane Preparedness Checklist
www.score.org/resource/hurricane-preparedness-checklist
This checklist will help you prepare for a hurricane's effect on your organization, employees and community by highlighting activities you should undertake before, during, and following the event.

Disaster Recovery Funding
www.fema.gov/media-library/assets/documents/134619
A wide range of federal, private, and non-profit funding, program and technical assistance resources that may be available pre and/or post disaster.

Disaster Loan Assistance
https://disasterloan.sba.gov/ela/Information/Index
SBA provides low-interest disaster loans to businesses of all sizes, private non-profit organizations, homeowners, and renters.

Disaster Unemployment Assistance
https://rafiusa.org/wp-content/uploads/2017/08/FACTSHEETDisasterUnemployment.pdf
The program provides unemployment benefits and reemployment services to individuals who have become unemployed as a result of a Presidential disaster declaration and are ineligible for regular state unemployment insurance.

About the Author

Maury Forman was the Senior Manager for the Washington State Department of Commerce until his retirement in 2016. His focus was on creating healthy communities and developing a culture of entrepreneurship in rural areas. He was the founder and director of the award-winning Northwest Economic Development course at Central Washington University. He became the first recipient of the Finkle Leadership award from the International Economic Development Council for his "integrity, tenacity, and philanthropic spirit in the profession."

Maury has won numerous awards for his workshops where he blended humor with education by creating Economic Development Jeopardy, Economic Developoly, Community Feud, Who Wants to be an Economic Developer? and the Site Selector Dating Game. Noah's Town is his 17th book about the profession but his first that does not include any cartoons. (well...except for the cover!)

Maury's blog posts can be found at www.MauryForum.com and startup.choosewashingtonstate.com

36907288R00075

Made in the USA
San Bernardino, CA
25 May 2019